Mastering Your Adult ADHD

✔**Treatments** *That Work*™

Mastering Your Adult ADHD

A COGNITIVE-BEHAVIORAL TREATMENT PROGRAM

Client Workbook

Steven A. Safren • Susan Sprich

Carol A. Perlman • Michael W. Otto

UNIVERSITY PRESS

2005

OXFORD
UNIVERSITY PRESS

Oxford University Press, Inc., publishes works that further
Oxford University's objective of excellence
in research, scholarship, and education.

Oxford   New York
Auckland   Cape Town   Dar es Salaam   Hong Kong   Karachi
Kuala Lumpur   Madrid   Melbourne   Mexico City   Nairobi
New Delhi   Shanghai   Taipei   Toronto

With offices in
Argentina   Austria   Brazil   Chile   Czech Republic   France   Greece
Guatemala   Hungary   Italy   Japan   Poland   Portugal   Singapore
South Korea   Switzerland   Thailand   Turkey   Ukraine   Vietnam

Copyright © 2005 by Oxford University Press, Inc.

Published by Oxford University Press, Inc.
198 Madison Avenue, New York, New York 10016

www.oup.com

Oxford is a registered trademark of Oxford University Press

9 8 7 6 5 4 3 2 1

Printed in the United States
on acid-free paper

About Treatments That Work™

One of the most difficult problems to confront patients with various disorders and diseases is how to find the best help available. Everyone is aware of friends or family who have sought treatment from a seemingly reputable practitioner, only to find out later from another doctor that the original diagnosis was wrong or the treatments recommended were inappropriate or perhaps even harmful. Most patients, or family members, address this problem by reading everything they can about their symptoms, seeking out information on the Internet, or aggressively "asking around" to tap knowledge from friends and acquaintances. Governments and health care policymakers are also aware that people in need don't always get the best treatments—something they refer to as "variability in health care practices."

Now health care systems around the world are attempting to correct this variability by introducing "evidence-based practice." This simply means that it is in everyone's interest that patients get the most up-to-date and effective care for a particular problem. Health care policymakers have also recognized that it is very useful to give consumers of health care as much information as possible so that they can make intelligent decisions in a collaborative effort to improve health and mental health. This series, "Treatments That Work™," is designed to accomplish just that. Only the latest and most effective interventions for particular problems are described in user-friendly language. To be included in this series, each treatment program must pass the highest standards of evidence available, as determined by a scientific advisory board. Thus, when individuals suffering from these problems or their family members seek out an expert clinician who is familiar with these interventions and decides that they are appropriate, they will have confidence that they are receiving the best care available. Of course, only your health care professional can decide on the right mix of treatments for you.

This particular program presents the first evidence-based effective psychological treatment for adult attention-deficit/hyperactivity disorder (ADHD). At present, it offers the best chance of experiencing some relief from this debilitating condition. In this program, you will learn skills that directly attack the three clusters of symptoms that make living with adult ADHD so difficult. These symptoms include difficulty focusing attention and being easily distracted, difficulties with organization and planning, and impulsivity. This program can be effectively combined with medications, or, for those 50 percent of individuals who derive relatively little benefit from medications, this program may be sufficient. This program is most effectively applied by working in collaboration with your clinician.

David H. Barlow, Editor-in-Chief,

Treatments That Work™

Boston, MA

Reference

Biederman, J., Wilens, T. E., Spencer, T. J., Farone, S., Mick, E., Ablon, J. S., & Keily, K. (1996). Diagnosis and treatment of adult attention-deficit/hyperactivity disorder. In M. Pollack & M. Otto & J. Rosenbaum (Eds.), *Challenges in clinical practice* (pp. 380–407). New York: Guilford Press.

Contents

Adaptive Thinking

Additional Skills

Information About Adult ADHD and This Treatment Program

Chapter 1   *Introduction*

Goals

- To understand the characteristics of ADHD in adulthood

- To learn why ADHD symptoms continue in adults even after treatment with medications

- To understand that ADHD is a valid diagnosis for adults

What Is ADHD?

Attention-deficit / hyperactivity disorder, or ADHD, is a valid, medical, psychiatric disorder. ADHD begins in childhood. However, many children with ADHD go on to have significant symptoms as adults.

As shown, people with ADHD have three major types of symptoms, which typically relate to

1. Poor attention

2. High impulsivity (or disinhibition)

3. High activity (hyperactivity)

Symptoms of Hyperactivity	**Symptoms of Poor Attention**	**Symptoms of Impulsivity**
Feel like driven by a motor	Easily distracted	Interrupt often
Restless	Difficulty organizing	Answer questions before person finishes asking them
Can't sit still	Becoming bored easily	Blurt out inappropriate comments
Always on the go	Difficulty switching from one task to another	Act before thinking
Fidgety	Difficulty planning	Do things you later regret
	Difficulty concentrating	Have difficulty waiting
	Can't do boring or unattractive tasks	

The term "disinhibition" (lack of inhibition) is also sometimes used to describe the impulsivity and hyperactivity symptoms. Many people with ADHD have at least some symptoms of poor attention, some symptoms of hyperactivity, and some symptoms of impulsivity; many people have symptoms that are predominately from one category.

The term "Attention Deficit Disorder," or ADD, is also sometimes used when an individual has the attentional symptoms but not the hyperactivity symptoms.

ADHD Is Not Related to Intelligence or Laziness

ADHD is a problem in which patients can learn coping skills to manage associated difficulties

Kate Kelly and Peggy Ramundo have written a self-help book for those with adult ADHD called *You Mean I'm Not Lazy, Stupid, or Crazy?* This title underscores many of the common misperceptions that people with ADHD have about themselves.

ADHD is a neurobiological disorder, unrelated to intelligence, laziness, aptitude, craziness, or anything similar. This program, which typically begins after stable medication treatment, can help control the symptoms of ADHD for adults. By actively learning skills and practicing them regularly, you will see significant improvements.

To diagnose a person with ADHD, mental health professionals use criteria set forth in the *Diagnostic and Statistical Manual of Mental Disorders*, published by the American Psychiatric Association (*DSM-IV*; APA 1994). Each of the following five criteria (A-E) must be met in order to qualify for a diagnosis of ADHD.

A. **Either six or more of the following symptoms of inattention or six or more of the following symptoms of hyperactivity/impulsivity must be present.**

Symptoms of Inattention	Symptoms of Hyperactivity/Impulsivity
Often fails to give close attention to details or makes careless mistakes in schoolwork, work, or other activities	Often fidgets with hands or feet or squirms in seat
Often has difficulty sustaining attention in tasks or play activities	Often leaves seat in classroom or in other situations in which remaining seated is expected
Often does not seem to listen when spoken to directly	Often runs about or climbs excessively in situations in which it is inappropriate (in adolescents or adults, may be limited to subjective feelings of restlessness)
Often does not follow through on instructions and fails to finish schoolwork, chores, or duties in the workplace (not because of oppositional behavior or failure to understand instructions)	Often has difficulty playing or engaging in leisure activities quietly
Often has difficulty organizing tasks and activities	Is often "on the go" or often acts as if "driven by a motor"
Often avoids, dislikes, or is reluctant to engage in tasks that require sustained mental effort	Often talks excessively
Often loses things necessary for tasks or activities	Often blurts out answers before questions have been completed
Is often easily distracted by extraneous stimuli	Often has difficulty awaiting turn
Is often forgetful in daily activities	Often interrupts or intrudes on others

B. Some symptoms were present before the age of 7.

C. Some impairment from the symptoms is present in two or more settings (e.g., work and home).

D. There must be clear evidence of clinically significant impairment in social, academic, or occupational functioning.

E. The symptoms do not occur exclusively during the course of a pervasive developmental disorder, schizophrenia, or other psychotic disorder and are not better accounted for by another mental disorder (e.g., mood disorder, anxiety disorder, dissociative disorder, or personality disorder).

How Do You Distinguish ADHD as a Diagnosis From Normal Functioning?

Some of the symptoms just listed sound like they might apply to almost anyone at certain times. For example, most people would probably say that they are sometimes easily distracted or sometimes have problems organizing. This is actually the case with many of the psychiatric disorders. For example, everyone gets sad sometimes, but not everyone suffers from a clinical diagnosis of depression.

This is why criteria C and D exist. In order to for ADHD to be considered as a medical diagnosis for any individual, he must have significant difficulties with some aspect of his life, such as work, significant relationship problems, and/or significant problems in school. These two criteria define the problem as significantly distressing to the person and as significantly interfering with some aspect of the person's life. "Significantly distressing" means that the problem causes emotional distress or pain. "Significantly interfering" means that the problem is somehow disruptive in a person's life, such as work, school, or relationships.

For ADHD to be the appropriate diagnosis, not only must the distress and impairment be present, but this distress and impairment must be caused by ADHD and not something else.

■ Cognitive components (thoughts and beliefs) can worsen ADHD symptoms. For example, a person who is facing something that feels overwhelming might shift her attention elsewhere or think things like "I can't do this," "I don't want to do this," or "I will do this later."

■ Behavioral components are the things people do that can exacerbate ADHD symptoms. The actual behaviors can include things like avoiding doing what you should be doing or not keeping an organizational system.

The model on the following page shows how we believe ADHD affects the lives of adults.

According to this model, the core symptoms of ADHD are biologically based. However, we believe that cognitive and behavioral variables also affect symptom levels.

Core neuropsychiatric impairments—starting in childhood—prevent effective coping. Adults with ADHD, by definition, have been suffering from this disorder chronically since childhood. Specific symptoms such as distractibility, disorganization, difficulty following through on tasks, and impulsivity can prevent people with ADHD from learning or using effective coping skills.

Lack of effective coping can lead to underachievement and failures. Because of this, patients with this disorder typically have sustained underachievement, or things that they might label "failures."

Underachievement and failures can lead to negative thoughts and beliefs. This history of failures can result in developing overly negative beliefs about oneself, as well as a habit of engaging in negative, maladaptive thinking when approaching tasks. The negative thoughts and beliefs that ensue can therefore add to avoidance or distractibility.

Negative thoughts and beliefs can lead to mood problems and can exacerbate avoidance. Therefore, people shift their attention even more when confronted with tasks or problems, and related behavioral symptoms can also get worse.

The following model (originally published in Safren et al., 2004) shows how these factors interrelate:

Cognitive-Behavioral Model of Adult ADHD

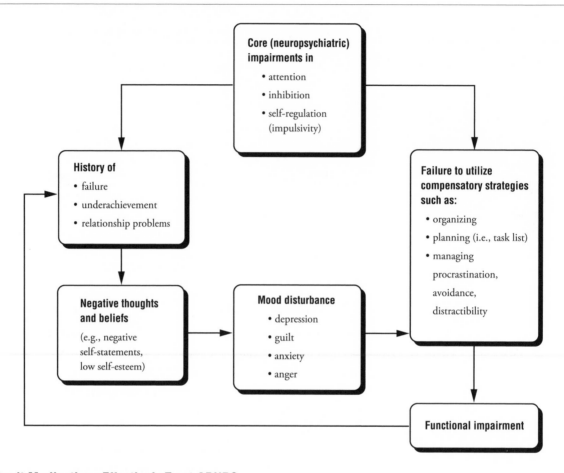

Core (neuropsychiatric) impairments in
• attention
• inhibition
• self-regulation (impulsivity)

History of
• failure
• underachievement
• relationship problems

Failure to utilize compensatory strategies such as:
• organizing
• planning (i.e., task list)
• managing procrastination, avoidance, distractibility

Negative thoughts and beliefs
(e.g., negative self-statements, low self-esteem)

Mood disturbance
• depression
• guilt
• anxiety
• anger

Functional impairment

Don't Medications Effectively Treat ADHD?

Yes.

Medications are currently the first-line treatment approach for adult ADHD, and they are the most extensively studied. The classes of these medications are stimulants, tricyclic antidepressants, monoamine oxidase inhibitors (antidepressants), and atypical antidepressants. However, a good number of individuals (approximately 20 to 50 percent) who take antidepressants are considered nonresponders. A nonresponder is an individual whose symptoms are not sufficiently reduced or who cannot tolerate the medications. Adults who are considered responders typically show a reduction in only 50 percent or less of the core symptoms of ADHD.

Because of these data, recommendations for the best treatment of adult ADHD include using psychotherapy (cognitive-behavior therapy, in particular) with medications. Medications can reduce many of the core symptoms of ADHD: attentional problems, high activity, and impulsivity.

If Medications Work, Why Have This Cognitive-Behavioral Treatment?

Medications do not intrinsically provide patients with concrete strategies and skills for coping.

Furthermore, disruptions in overall quality of life such as underachievement, unemployment or underemployment, economic problems, and relationship difficulties associated with ADHD in adulthood call for the application of additional ameliorative interventions.

Evidence That ADHD in Adulthood Is a Real and Valid Medical Condition

We include this section here because in the recent past, ADHD was a controversial diagnosis.

However, the past 15 years of study have shown that its validity is strong. We will describe the controversy regarding the diagnosis and outline the evidence that has led experts to conclude that it is a prevalent, distressing, and impairing, valid medical diagnosis.

Psychiatric and psychological diagnoses are difficult to validate compared to other biomedical diseases. ADHD in adulthood is a real, reliably diagnosed medical illness that may affect up to 5 percent of the adult population in the United States. ADHD in adulthood has historically been a controversial diagnosis. One of the reasons for this is that psychiatric diagnoses, in general, are difficult to validate. In many other medical fields, doctors can perform a blood test, do an x-ray, do a biopsy, or even take a patient's temperature in order to inform a diagnosis. In these cases, overt medical evidence complements the report of the patient. However, for psychiatric disorders, this is presently impossible. Doctors must diagnose psychiatric disorders on the basis of only the report of patient's symptoms, their own observation of the patient, or the observations of others. Therefore, psychiatrists and psychologists have developed a way to categorize psychiatric disorders that involves the presentation of clusters of symptoms that people have.

How do doctors validate psychological or psychiatric diagnoses? In order to validate a psychiatric or psychological diagnosis, psychologists and psychiatrists therefore examine data such as the degree to which trained individuals agree on diagnosis, the degree to which the disorder runs in families (including adoption studies to determine the relative impact of biology versus one's environment), any neuroimaging and neurochemistry studies, and the degree to which people who have the problem experience distress. This has been done sufficiently for adult ADHD.

How do we know that ADHD is a real diagnosis? Sufficient scientific evidence has accumulated over the past 15 years converging on the finding that ADHD is a real, significant, distressing, interfering, and legitimate medical problem. This includes evidence that ADHD can be reliably diagnosed in adults and that the diagnosis meets standards of diagnostic validity similar to those of other psychiatric diagnoses. Accordingly, core symptoms in adulthood include impairments in attention, inhibition, and self-regulation. These core symptoms yield associated impairments in adulthood such as poor school and work performance (e.g., poor organizational and planning skills; a tendency to become bored easily; deficient sustained attention to reading and paperwork; procrastination; poor time management; impulsive decision making); impaired interpersonal skills (problems with friendships; poor follow-through on commitments; poor listening skills; difficulty with intimate relationships); and behavior problems (lower level of educational attainment than would be expected for level of ability; poor financial management; trouble organizing one's home; chaotic routine). There is further evidence for the validity of ADHD as a diagnosis from medication treatment studies, genetic studies that include adoption and family studies, and neuroimaging and neurochemistry research.

Children with ADHD do grow up. Estimates of the prevalence of ADHD in adulthood range from 1 to 5 percent. This is consistent with estimates that ADHD affects 2 to 9 percent of school-age children, and follow-up studies of children diagnosed with ADHD showing that impairing ADHD symptoms persist into adulthood in 30 to 80 percent of diagnosed children.

Chapter 2 | *Overview of the Program*

Goals

- To learn how this program was developed

- To learn about the concerns of medication-treated adults with ADHD

- To understand the success rate of the program so far

- To understand what the program will involve

This treatment program is meant to be completed with the assistance of a cognitive-behavioral therapist. The treatment was developed by the Massachusetts General Hospital's Cognitive-Behavioral Therapy Program. It was based on the clinical experience of the authors, input from adults living with ADHD, and published works on treatment for adults with ADHD (e.g., Barkley, 1998; Hallowell, 1995; Mayes 1998; McDermott, 2000; Nadeau, 1995). It is designed for patients who have been diagnosed with ADHD, have been on medications for ADHD, and have found a stable medication regimen. The strategies may be useful for adults with ADHD who cannot take medications; however, we have tested it only for individuals who were already taking medications.

How Was the Program Developed?

Clinical experience of the authors. The program was developed by a group of psychologists at Massachusetts General Hospital and Harvard Medical School after treating patients with ADHD in our clinic using cognitive-behavioral therapy. From this perspective, it was originally developed from the clinical experience of the authors, general principles of cognitive-behavioral therapy, and published clinical guidelines for working with adult patients with ADHD.

Input from adults living with ADHD. Patients with ADHD also gave input to the development of the treatment program. One of the authors interviewed a group of patients with ADHD who had been taking medications and obtained their views regarding the types of problems they were experiencing and what they felt would be helpful regarding cognitive-behavioral treatment.

The most frequently discussed problems among adult patients with ADHD who had been taking medicines were (1) organizing and planning, (2) distractibility, and (3) associated anxiety and depression. Other concerns included problems with procrastination, anger management, and communication issues. Examples are discussed below.

Organizing and Planning

Problems with organizing and planning involve difficulties figuring out the logical, discrete steps to complete tasks that seem overwhelming. For many patients, this leads to giving up, procrastination, anxiety, and feelings of incompetence and underachievement.

We have had, for example, several patients who were underemployed or unemployed who had never done thorough job searches. This resulted in their not having a job, working in a much lower-paying position than they could have, or not having a job that would lead to appropriate employment.

Distractibility

The problems with distractibility involved problems in work or school. Many of our patients have reported that they do not complete tasks because other, less important things get in the way.

Examples might include sitting down at one's computer to work on a project but constantly going on the Internet to look up certain Web sites or browsing items on eBay. We had a student in our program who lived alone; whenever he sat down to do his thesis, he would find another place in his apartment to clean (even though it was already clean enough).

Mood Problems (Associated Anxiety and Depression)

In association with core ADHD symptoms, many of our patients have mood problems.

These problems involve worry about events in their lives and sadness regarding either real underachievement or perceived underachievement. Many individuals with ADHD report a strong sense of frustration about tasks that they do not finish or tasks that they complete less well than they feel they should or could have.

Has This Program Been Successful?

Yes!

In our study of this treatment, we found that people who completed this program in addition to taking their medications did significantly better than people who stayed on their medications but did not receive this treatment (Safren et al., in press).

We conducted a "randomized controlled trial" to find these results. Randomized controlled trials are a primary way researchers test whether treatments work. They are randomized in that patients entering the study randomly receive either the treatment or a control condition.

In our study, we took in only patients who had been treated with medications but still had significant problems. These patients were randomized to either getting the treatment described in this book or no additional treatment (all patients continued on their prescribed medications).

In this study, the people who got the treatment had significantly lower symptoms of ADHD after the treatment. This was evaluated by an independent assessor who did not know whether the participants got the treatment or not and by the self-report of participants who completed written questionnaires about their symptoms. According to these assessments, patients who got the program experienced about a 50 percent decrease in symptoms, and those who did not had negligible changes.

The program will entail regular meetings with a therapist and homework. The treatment involves regular meetings with a cognitive-behavioral therapist and homework assignments. We have found that weekly sessions work best. By having weekly sessions, you have a chance to practice the skills discussed in the treatment in the time between your meetings with your therapist. Also, there is a relatively short period of time between sessions, so any problems with follow-through can be solved and any questions about the approach can be answered. When we have conducted sessions every other week, patients reported that they found it difficult because they would forget what they were supposed to be doing on their own.

The treatment is different than traditional psychotherapy. In fact, in some ways it is more like taking a course than being in supportive psychotherapy. Each session will have an agenda, and each session will involve a homework assignment. Practice is essential.

The program involves practicing outside the sessions! There are no two ways about it! We have found that many patients have tried similar strategies in the past but have had difficulties integrating this practice in their daily life. In other words, the tendency to be distractible and forgetful can get in the way of treatment. We will work with you to "set in" new habits that you can keep with you over the years

You will need to practice these new skills long enough for them to become a habit—for them to be easy to use and remember.

You will be tempted to quit, but not at the beginning. At the beginning, things will be novel and new and therefore more interesting. People typically do not quit at the beginning. The middle period can sometimes be the hardest. This is the time when the novelty wears off but people have not practiced the skills long enough for them to become habits. Many people show some improvement at the beginning, enough improvement that they start to think that they do not need to use the skills. In this case, people quit because the work is no longer new and interesting and is not yet an easy habit; they then relapse back to having problems and then think, "I tried to change, and I could not do it." Hence, the cycle of negative emotions and continued ADHD symptoms continues.

■ *Do not succumb to this temptation.* ■

This may be the hardest part of the treatment program. The key to getting better is to stay on track, keep with the program long enough for it to be easy, and practice.

The program will entail ups and downs; sometimes it will entail setbacks. When there is a "down," this is definitely not a time to quit; this is a time to learn from the things that led up to the setback, and to figure out how to handle them in the future. This is extremely important.

■ *Setbacks are a major part of progress. You need to have setbacks and learn to handle them in order to reduce the likelihood of future setbacks!* ■

The final period is easier; however, it also entails challenges. Once things are going better, you will be faced with the challenge of continuing to invest some time and energy to maintaining these systems and skills even though things are going better.

We have found that some people, once they are doing better, feel less motivated to keep using the coping skills. If things are bad, then there is more motivation because people feel that they need to "get out of the hole."

The Program Will Entail Different Modules

Organization and Planning

The first part of the treatment involves organization and planning skills. This includes skills such as:

- Learning to effectively and consistently use a calendar book

- Learning to effectively and consistently use a task list

- Working on effective problem-solving skills, including (1) breaking down tasks into steps and (2) choosing a best solution for a problem when no solution is ideal

- Figuring out a system for organizing and responding to mail and papers

Managing Distractibility

The second part of treatment involves managing distractibility. Skills and strategies include the following:

■ Maximizing and building on one's attentions span (breaking tasks into steps that correspond to the length of one's attention span, then working to expand this strategy)

■ Using a timer, cues, and other techniques to help reduce the effects of distractibility

Using Adaptive Thinking

The third part of treatment involves learning to think about problems and stressors in the most adaptive way possible. This includes:

■ Positive "self-coaching"

■ Learning how to identify and dispute negative thoughts

■ Learning how to look at situations rationally, and therefore make rational choices about the best possible solutions for you

Application to Procrastination

An optional additional module exists for procrastination. We include this because most of the previous modules do relate to procrastination, but some people require extra help in this area. This module therefore specifically points to how to use the skills already learned to help with procrastination.

Before starting this program, your doctor will likely have done a diagnostic interview to establish whether or not you have ADHD. Part of the treatment approach described in this workbook involves regularly monitoring your improvement. Because, unlike many medical illnesses, we do not have a blood test for symptom severity, we need to use the next best thing, which is the ADHD Symptom Severity Scale, which is included on page 23. You should complete this around the time of your first session. We recommend completing it each week thereafter so that you can monitor your progress and so that you can target areas that may not be improving at the rate you would like.

The program will entail setting an agenda for each treatment session. In order to ensure that important material is covered, each session corresponds to the material presented in this workbook.

One potential pitfall with modular treatment is that not everything can be covered at once. Although the treatment approach is offered one module at a time, patients may have areas of difficulty that will not be addressed until future sessions.

This is another issue that is sometimes frustrating for people who do this program. The program typically starts with the development of a calendar and task list system. This module also involves learning organization and planning skills. The next module targets distractibility. People sometimes have problems with the first module because they get easily distracted, but distractibility is not covered until the next module. Unfortunately, it is impossible to learn everything all at once, so we ask that you do your best, but realize that you will not have learned all the necessary skills until the end of the treatment program.

The Program Will Entail Repetition

There are many areas of the treatment where we repeat key information. We do this because repetition is the best way to learn new information. Each module contains new information but also contains information from previous modules that are important to review.

For some people with ADHD, taking medication every day, sometimes more than once a day, can be difficult. Symptoms of ADHD such as distractibility or poor organization may interfere, causing you to forget to take all of your prescribed doses or to have difficulty developing a structured routine for taking medication. This treatment will help you prioritize taking medication and will provide you with opportunities to work with a therapist and problem-solve around difficulties taking medications. Each week you will discuss factors that have led you to miss doses.

Chapter 3   *Involvement of Your Family Member*

Overview

This single chapter will assist you in working with a family member to better manage your ADHD symptoms. As has been discussed earlier, this treatment program is best done with the aid of a therapist who is familiar with cognitive-behavioral therapy. We therefore recommend that you and your partner meet with the therapist for one session to go over the material presented in the first two chapters and to deal with any other information that may be pertinent.

Involving a family member in treatment will enable you to:

- Gain support as you complete treatment

- Decrease tension in your relationship related to ADHD symptoms

Goals

- To provide education about ADHD

- To discuss ways in which ADHD has affected your relationship with a family member

- To provide an overview of the CBT model of the continuation of ADHD into adulthood

- To discuss organization and planning techniques

- To discuss techniques for coping with distractibility

- To discuss adaptive thinking techniques

Review of Symptom Severity Scale

As you have been doing each week, you should complete the ADHD self-report symptom checklist. Be sure to review your score and take note of symptoms that have improved and those that are still problematic.

Score:_____

Date:_____

Review of Medication Adherence

As you have been doing each week, you should record your prescribed dosage of medication and indicate the number of doses you missed. Review triggers for missed doses, such as distractibility, running out of medication, or thoughts about not wanting/needing to take medication.

Prescribed doses per week: _____

Doses missed this week: _____

Triggers for missed doses: _____

_____

_____

Review of Material From Chapters 1 and 2

The information presented in the previous two chapters can be shared with your partner or spouse. This information lays the groundwork for the remaining sessions. We recommend that this be discussed with your cognitive-behavioral therapist, who can answer questions that your partner might have.

ADHD can certainly contribute to strained relationships with family members, especially when they are not familiar with the symptoms of ADHD and associated difficulties. Both you and your partner should answer each of the following questions separately and then compare the responses.

Client Responses

What are the symptoms of ADHD that you think are most significant?

_____

_____

_____

What are the three most important ways that these symptoms have affected the relationship?

1. _____

_____

2. _____

_____

3. _____

_____

Family Member Responses

What are the symptoms of ADHD in your partner that bother you most?

_____

_____

_____

What are the three most important ways that these symptoms have affected the relationship?

1. _____

_____

2. _____

_____

3. _____

_____

Monitoring Progress

Each week we monitor progress by completion of the ADHD symptom rating scale. We find that this is helpful to identify areas that are most problematic and areas that should be targeted for additional work.

We also sometimes ask the family member to complete a symptom rating scale as a secondary way to report on progress. If you are willing, we would like to have the family member complete one, and we can compare ratings to see if problematic areas are similar.

This measure is included in this workbook. To obtain a total score, add all of the ratings. Use 0 for items rated "never or rarely," 1 for items rated "sometimes," 2 for items rated "often," and 3 for items rated "very often."

Current Symptoms Self-Report Form

Week of:

Instructions: Please check the response next to each item that best describes your behavior *during the past week.*

		Never or Rarely	Sometimes	Often	Very Often
1	Fail to give close attention to details or make careless mistakes in my work				
2	Fidget with hands or feet or squirm in seat				
3	Have difficulty sustaining my attention in tasks or fun activities				
4	Leave my seat in situations in which seating is expected				
5	Don't listen when spoken to directly				
6	Feel restless				
7	Don't follow through on instructions and fail to finish work				
8	Have difficulty engaging in leisure activities or doing fun things quietly				
9	Have difficulty organizing tasks and activities				
10	Feel "on the go" or "driven by a motor"				
11	Avoid, dislike, or am reluctant to engage in work that requires sustained mental effort				
12	Talk excessively				
13	Lose things necessary for tasks or activities				
14	Blurt out answers before questions have been completed				
15	Am easily distracted				
16	Have difficulty awaiting turn				
17	Am forgetful in daily activities				
18	Interrupt or intrude on others				

From R. A. Barkley & K. R. Murphy (1998), *Attention-Deficit Hyperactivity Disorder: A clinical workbook* (2nd ed.). New York: Guilford Press.

Current Symptoms Family Member Report Form

Instructions: Please check the response next to each item that best describes your family member's behavior *during the past week.*

		Never or Rarely	Sometimes	Often	Very Often
1	Fails to give close attention to details or makes careless mistakes in work				
2	Fidgets with hands or feet or squirms in seat				
3	Has difficulty sustaining attention in tasks or fun activities				
4	Leaves seat in situations in which seating is expected				
5	Doesn't listen when spoken to directly				
6	Feels restless				
7	Doesn't follow through on instructions and fails to finish work				
8	Has difficulty engaging in leisure activities or doing fun things quietly				
9	Has difficulty organizing tasks and activities				
10	Feels "on the go" or "driven by a motor"				
11	Avoids, dislikes, or is reluctant to engage in work that requires sustained mental effort				
12	Talks excessively				
13	Loses things necessary for tasks or activities				
14	Blurts out answers before questions have been completed				
15	Is easily distracted				
16	Has difficulty awaiting turn				
17	Is forgetful in daily activities				
18	Interrupts or intrudes on others				

Adapted from R. A. Barkley & K. R. Murphy (1998), *Attention-Deficit Hyperactivity Disorder: A clinical workbook* (2nd ed.). New York: Guilford Press.

Organization and Planning

Chapter 4   *The Foundation: Organization and Planning Skills*

Goals

- ▓ To understand the severity of your initial symptoms as a basis for tracking treatment progress

- ▓ To discuss realistic goals

- ▓ To learn about the modular approach to treatment, and the importance of practice, motivation, and staying with it

- ▓ To be introduced to using a notebook and calendar system

- ▓ Homework: To get started with a notebook and calendar system

Review of Symptom Severity Scale

The ADHD Symptom Severity Scale, on page 23, lists each of the diagnostic symptoms of ADHD to help you rate yourself. A total score can be obtained by summing all of the ratings. Use 0 for all items rated "never or rarely," 1 for all items rated "sometimes," 2 for all items rated "often," and 3 for all items rated "very often."

Each week of treatment, we will target specific symptoms from this assessment. As you go through the treatment, you should expect to see a gradual decline in symptom severity. If there are specific sets of symptoms that do not seem to be changing, these are areas on which you should focus.

Tracking your symptoms on a weekly basis can also help you become more aware of these difficulties. Being aware that these are symptoms of ADHD, doing this self assessment on a weekly basis, and tracking the changes can also be helpful on its own. This awareness can help you remember to use the skills that you will be learning in the sessions that follow.

Complete the ADHD self-report symptom checklist. Pay particular attention to the items that have the highest ratings; these should be targets for goals of treatment.

Score:_____

Date:_____

Review of Medication Adherence

As you have been doing each week, you should record your prescribed dosage of medication and indicate the number of doses you missed. Review triggers for missed doses, such as distractibility, running out of medication, or thoughts about not wanting/needing to take medication.

Prescribed doses per week: _____

Doses missed this week: _____

Triggers for missed doses: _____

_____

_____

Goals for Cognitive-Behavioral Therapy for ADHD

You have just completed a checklist of the symptoms that are typical of ADHD in adults. We find that reviewing this list can also help you think about individual goals that you might have regarding which types of problems most affect you. Additionally, it might help you think about how they actually interfere in your life.

Part of getting started on this course of cognitive-behavioral therapy for ADHD is making sure you have realistic goals for the treatment.

Realistic goals for cognitive-behavioral therapy for ADHD are things that you can control. You might be thinking that a long-term (or medium-term) goal of yours is to get a better job. This is a great goal, and we believe the skills described in this workbook can help you increase the chances of getting a better job. However, the outcome of getting a better job is dependent on lots of other factors that you do not directly control (such as the economy and the availability of the types of jobs you want). A realistic goal would therefore be to figure out what steps are necessary to improve the chances to get a better job, and to act on these steps.

There are likely areas related to ADHD that are also preventing you from getting a better job. These might include figuring out an effective job search process, improving your organizational skills at work, and improving your productivity. These are issues that the treatment can help with because we can directly control them.

Questions to Help Come Up with Goals

The following questions may be helpful with respect to coming up with goals regarding your treatment.

What made you decide to start this treatment now?

What types of things would you like to be different regarding how you approach tasks?

What are some issues that others have noticed about how you approach things?

If you did not have problems with ADHD, what do you think would be different?

In the following table, write down your goals for cognitive-behavioral therapy. There are columns for controllability and whether the goal is short or long term. For controllability, write down how much control you think you would have over this goal if the ADHD symptoms were gone (0 percent represents no control; 100 percent represents complete control). Also indicate whether this is a short-term or long-term goal.

Goal List

Goal of CBT	Controllability (as a percentage)	Short or Long Term

We ask you to rate controllability (and this should be done with a therapist) so that you can gain a realistic appraisal of your goals for CBT. For example, a goal might be to get a job. However, as we have noted, there are many factors involved in getting a job. Therefore, we prefer to have a related goal that is more controllable—for example, to complete the tasks that are necessary to optimize the chances of getting a job.

Re-review the goals and the controllability ratings. Ask yourself if there are specific areas that you can control about each situation and if there are specific areas that are beyond your control.

As we have discussed, this treatment is modular. In other words, it is designed so that each skill builds upon previously learned skills. So you will learn one technique at a time. As you begin this treatment program, there are several things to keep in mind about how the treatment is structured.

The therapy is active. First, due to difficulties known to be associated with ADHD, the therapy will be especially active, almost like taking a course. Each session will have an agenda, which you and your therapist will discuss at the beginning.

The therapy requires homework. Each session will involve a review of the things you have already learned and are working on, as well as a discussion of new coping strategies. You will also be expected to try them out over the next week. The more you are able to do this, the better the results you will see.

The therapy works on one skill at a time. This means that you will have areas of difficulty that are not addressed right away. For example, the first module is on organizing and planning. The second is on distractibility. Of course, organizing and planning things is much easier if you do not become distracted. Likewise, if we started with distractibility, it would be difficult to figure out what you were getting distracted from if you are not organized. Therefore, it is important to realize that only one thing at a time can be changed, and the key is to practice things long enough so that you can really tell if they will be helpful to you.

Practice Makes Perfect

You are about to start a treatment for problems that involve difficulties with follow-through. Some or all of these skills may seem difficult. This is why you will be practicing them with a therapist and not on your own, and is also why it is critical to know right from the start how important practicing these new skills is. Remember the model that is in the previous chapter. Many people with ADHD never get a chance to learn coping skills because they quit before they have practiced them enough for them to become a habit!

Because motivation is so important for this treatment, the following exercise is a way to help you figure out whether this program is for you and to resolve any ambivalence about completing it.

This exercise is a good one to keep and review again as you continue in treatment. As discussed earlier, going through the program is likely to involve some ups and some downs. You may or may not notice benefits right away, but as you move through the exercises, keep in mind that you are developing new strategies that are aimed at both current and future patterns of behavior. As you do this exercise, be sure to keep in mind the important long-term benefits.

Motivational Exercise: Pros and Cons of Changing

Therapy will ask you to try new things and, at times, to try strategies you have tried in the past. Also, homework will be assigned following each session, and this homework is aimed at having you do things differently from your usual habit. The result of a new therapy like this is that, at least for a while, you will need to leave your natural "comfort zone" and try things in a new way. As you prepare to try things in a new way, it will be helpful for you to keep in mind the natural difficulties you will have with change, as well as the potential benefits. For example, when you think about trying a new organizational system, you may think, "I hate the idea of getting a notebook. I have had one in the past, and it didn't work for me; I just ended up with page after page of lists that I did not complete."

Accordingly, one of the "cons" of trying the notebook system is that you face old thoughts and old memories about how notebooks may not work. On the other hand, it is quite possible that the way in which the notebook system is applied in this therapy at this time may have benefit. So a "pro" about trying the notebook system again is that it may have some important features that might lead to success at the present time.

As you go through the rest of the chapter, notice ways in which you may be reluctant to try the new system. Then come back to the following page and list some of the pros and cons that trying new behaviors may bring. Space is provided for considering two new strategies.

Motivational Exercise: Pros and Cons of Changing

New Strategy to Be Considered

	PRO	CON
Short-term consequences		
Long-term consequences		

New Strategy to Be Considered

	PRO	CON
Short-term consequences		
Long-term consequences		

Skill: Using a Calendar and Notebook

Having a calendar and notebook system is the foundation of being organized. It is absolutely necessary. Although there are other things also necessary, this is critical. We consider it akin to eating.

In order to maintain your health, you need to be able to eat. However, there are many other things that you also need to do to maintain your health, such as go to the doctor, go on medicines if you get an infection, and so on. Eating is a necessary but not sufficient requirement for health. We believe that maintaining a calendar and notebook system is necessary but not sufficient for being organized.

Using the Calendar and Notebook Together

The calendar system and notebook systems can be personalized, though we give specific recommendations. Many individuals report that they have tried to use a calendar system in the past but it has not worked, or they did not keep up with it. Remember, the goal of this treatment is to try things long enough for them to become habits. Every week from here on in involves learning tasks that build on the use of the calendar and notebook system. These two items can be used together.

The notebook will contain information you need but that is not tied to a specific date, including things like recording phone messages, directions to places, and to-do list items. The notebook should replace random pieces of paper that can be easily lost.

The calendar is your key to appointments. When using the calendar with the notebook, you may place items from the to-do list onto specific days or times.

Rules for the Calendar and Notebook

1. **The calendar and notebook replaces ALL pieces of paper.**

   ▓ Pieces of paper just get lost.

   ▓ Instead of keeping an appointment slip, a business card, or anything of this sort, copy the information into the notebook. When the notebook is full, you can replace it.

2. **Phone messages from voice mail or other places go in the notebook.**

   ▓ All phone messages (e.g.,from voice mail) get logged into the notebook as a to-do item.

   ▓ If you keep the notebooks after they are full, you can refer back to them if you need someone's number in the future.

   ▓ If you enter the date when the tasks are completed, you will have a record of your work, in case anyone asks you about it in the future.

3. **All appointments go in the notebook.**

   ▥ No appointment slips that can easily get lost!

4. **The notebook must contain a to-do list.**

   ▥ The to-do list is something that will be further developed in future chapters. This is a key component of the program.

   ▥ To-do list items should be looked at every day and revised as necessary.

   ▥ When it gets messy, recopy the list.

5. **Do not obsess trying to get a perfect system.**

   ▥ Many individuals want to have the perfect calendar and to-do list system. Do not fall into this trap. This will just result in not having a system.

   ▥ If you cannot decide on the "best" system, then just use a simple calendar book and, separately, a regular notebook.

   ▥ Remember, it's important to give your system a fair shot! This means keeping one system for at least three months, long enough to get used to it.

6. **If you have difficulty with computers, do not try to use a computerized system.**

   ▥ Many individuals feel that they want to start using a computerized or PDA system. This works wonderfully for individuals who are already proficient with computers. If this is not you, this is not the time to start.

   ▥ If you are not proficient with computers, you can always try to become proficient at the end of this treatment. We recommend that this be a separate goal from this program, however. Either learn to use a computer before starting the program or do so afterward.

It is important to remember that learning any new skill takes practice, and takes time. You may not be used to writing down appointments or carrying around a calendar or notebook. Be aware of thoughts that may sabotage your success down the road:

"I don't have room in my bag for a calendar."

"It's a hassle to have to bring a notebook everywhere with me."

"I've never been an organized person, so why start now?"

"If I write down my appointments and assignments, I will then be responsible for them."

You will be learning ways to manage these interfering thoughts in later chapters. For now, try to keep focused on your reasons for beginning this program, the goals you hope to achieve, and the accomplishment you will feel for taking positive steps in your life.

Homework

✎ Begin using a calendar and notebook system following the rules given in this chapter.

✎ Bring in the calendar and task list to the next treatment session.

Chapter 5 *Organization of Multiple Tasks*

The main focus of this session is to teach you how to manage multiple tasks. It is important for you to remember that practice makes perfect.

Although these techniques may seem unfamiliar at first, over time they will become more automatic. Even if you feel frustrated, it is important for you to stick with the techniques until they become habits.

Goals

- To continue to monitor your progress

- To review your use of the calendar and task list

- To learn how to manage multiple tasks

- To learn how to prioritize tasks

- To problem-solve regarding any anticipated difficulties using this technique

- To identify exercises for home practice

Review of Symptom Severity Scale

As you have been doing each week, you should complete the ADHD self-report symptom checklist. Be sure to review your score and take note of symptoms that have improved and those that are still problematic.

Score:_____

Date:_____

Review of Medication Adherence

As you have been doing each week, you should record your prescribed dosage of medication and indicate the number of doses you missed. Review triggers for missed doses, such as distractibility, running out of medication, or thoughts about not wanting/needing to take medication.

Prescribed doses per week: _____

Doses missed this week: _____

Triggers for missed doses: _____

_____

_____

Review of Previous Modules

Each week you should examine your progress in implementing skills from each of the previous modules. It is important to acknowledge the successes you have achieved and to problem-solve around any difficulties.

Review: Tools for Organization and Planning

■ Calendar for managing appointments

■ Notebook for recording a to-do list

Homework Review

Remember, having a good calendar and task list system is necessary (but not sufficient) for getting organized.

If you have not yet purchased a notebook or calendar book, find a way to get one immediately.

Remember, problem-solving skills are covered in future sessions. However, before actually getting to those sessions, try to figure out how to problem-solve getting a calendar and notebook. If necessary and possible, purchase one right now. In order for this approach to be successful, it is imperative that you have the proper tools!

If you have obtained a calendar book and notebook system, review specifics:

▨ Where you will keep the book?

▨ How will you remember to use it every day?

▨ How will you remember to look at your task list every day? (We find that picking a time every day is the best—for example, when you feed your dog, after you brush your teeth, while you are having your morning coffee or breakfast.)

Remember, just because you have a to-do list, it doesn't mean that you have to complete all of the items on the list immediately! It is simply a tool that is going to help you become organized and avoid forgetting things that you have not written down.

▨ *The calendar and task lists are building blocks for the rest of the treatment program. Make sure to plan a strategy to look at them EVERY DAY!* ▨

In the task list and the calendar, you may have noticed that we often need to manage multiple tasks at one time. When you have ADHD, it can become difficult to decide which task is most important. Even when you have decided that a particular task is important, it is often difficult to stick with it until it is completed.

In the following exercise, you will learn a concrete strategy to help you decide which tasks are most important. This technique is one example of how you can force yourself to organize tasks even though it is difficult for people with ADHD to process this type of information.

Skill: Prioritizing

When you are faced with a number of tasks that you must do, it is important to have a clear strategy for prioritizing which tasks are most important so that you make sure that you complete the most important tasks.

The best way that we know of to do this is to rate each task.

We find that people like to complete the tasks that are easier but less important first. This can be problematic. When we do this, we get the feeling that we are getting things accomplished but find that we are never making progress on our important goals.

Skill: The A, B, Cs

Use the "A," "B," and "C" ratings. We have found that it works best to list all of the tasks first and then assign the priority ratings.

"A" Tasks: These are the tasks of highest importance. This means that they must be completed in the short term (like today or tomorrow).

"B" Tasks: These are tasks of less importance, to be done over the long term. Some portions of the task should be completed in the short term, but the other portions may take longer.

"C" Tasks: These tasks, of the lowest importance, may be more attractive and easier to do but are not as important as tasks with higher rankings.

In this chapter, you should generate a task list, and discuss ratings for each item. Be very careful not to rate too many items as A!

You can now add this technique to your "tool box" of skills that you are developing to combat your ADHD symptoms. In addition to making a to-do list for each day, you should now assign a rating of "A," "B," or "C" to each task. You should do *all* of the "A" tasks before doing *any* of the "B" tasks!! This may be hard for you, but it is very important! It will help you to make sure that you complete the tasks that are important to you.

■ *Use this technique every day. Make a new list when the old one becomes too messy to read easily.* ■

Potential Pitfalls

You may be feeling that we are asking you to do a lot.

Don't get discouraged!

You are trying to learn some new skills, and it will take some time before the skills become habits. As you become more accustomed to writing down your to-do list, you will learn more about how much is realistic for you to expect to do in one day.

At this point, if you find that you are not finishing all of the items on your list, simply re-rate them the next day. In later chapters, you may want to problem-solve if you are finding that you are consistently not finishing the most important items on your list.

Remember, at this point, you are just trying to get in the habit of using the to-do list.

✎ Use your notebook every day to maintain your to-do list.

✎ Use and look at your task list and calendar EVERY DAY!

✎ Rate each task "A," "B," or "C."

✎ Practice doing all of the "A" tasks before the "B" tasks and all of the "B" tasks before the "C" tasks (for this reason, there should be fewer A tasks than B or C tasks).

✎ Carry over tasks that are not completed; cross out the ones that are completed.

✎ Consider any difficulties that you anticipate may interfere with your completing your homework.

An example of a task list is provided on page 43. See if you like this format for your task list.

Task List

Priority Rating	Task	Date Put on List	Date Completed
A			
.			
.			
.			
.			
.			
.			
B			
.			
.			
.			
.			
.			
.			
C			
.			
.			
.			
.			
.			

Chapter 6

Problem-Solving and Managing Overwhelming Tasks

The main skills that you will learn in this session are how to solve problems effectively and how to take a task that, at first, seems overwhelming and break it down into manageable steps. The problem-solving techniques are adapted from cognitive-behavioral interventions that focus exclusively on problem-solving (e.g., D'Zurilla, 1986; Nezu, Nezu, Friedman, Faddis, & Houts, 1998).

Goals

- To continue to monitor your progress

- To review your use of the calendar and task list, particularly the A, B, and C priority ratings

- To learn how to use problem-solving to overcome difficulties with task completion or selection of a solution

- To learn how to break a large task into manageable steps

- To troubleshoot difficulties using this technique

- To identify exercises for home practice

Review of Symptom Severity Scale

As you have been doing each week, you should complete the ADHD self-report symptom checklist. Be sure to review your score and take note of symptoms that have improved and those that are still problematic.

Score:_____

Date:_____

Review of Medication Adherence

As you have been doing each week, you should record your prescribed dosage of medication and indicate the number of doses you missed. Review triggers for missed doses, such as distractibility, running out of medication, or thoughts about not wanting/needing to take medication.

Prescribed doses per week: _____

Doses missed this week: _____

Triggers for missed doses: _____

_____

_____

Review of Previous Modules

Each week you should review your progress in implementing skills from each of the previous modules. It is important to acknowledge the successes you have achieved and problem-solve around any difficulties.

Review: Tools for Organization and Planning

- Calendar for managing appointments
- Notebook for recording a to-do list
- Use of the "A," "B," and "C" priority ratings

In this section, we focus on learning to recognize when you are having difficulty completing a task or are becoming overwhelmed and cannot figure out exactly where to start. The reason we call problems "problems" is that there is no easy solution at hand; usually any solution has serious pros and cons.

This typically can lead to problems like procrastination.

Once you recognize that there is a problem, you can use these problem-solving strategies to help.

We are going to go over two skills that may seem simple but are actually quite powerful.

The two skills are:

1. Selecting an action plan

2. Breaking down an overwhelming task into manageable steps

Developing an action plan can be helpful when it is difficult to determine how to resolve a problem or when the number of possible solutions becomes overwhelming. Selecting an action plan involves the five steps in problem-solving listed here.

Use these instructions in conjunction with the sheet on page 49.

1. **Articulate the problem.**

    Try to describe the problem in as few words as possible—one to two sentences at the most. Examples are "I cannot decide whether I should quit my job" and "I cannot decide what to do about a coworker whom I can't stand."

2. **List all possible solutions.**

    In these columns you want to try to figure all of the different solutions, regardless of how possible they are, what the consequences may be, or whether or not they sound outrageous. The idea is to really generate a list of as many solutions as possible.

3. **List the pros and cons of each solution.**

    Now is the time to realistically appraise each solution. In these columns you want to figure out what you really think would happen if you picked that solution. List the pros (advantages) and cons (disadvantages) of each.

4. **Rate each solution.**

    Using the final column, rate the pros and cons of the solution on a scale from 1 to 10. Try to be as objective as possible, but include the relative difficulty it would take. For example, if one solution is to assertively say no to something, you should factor in whether this will be anxiety provoking, as well as whether it will have the desired outcome.

5. **Implement the best option.**

    Now that you have rated each option on a scale of 1 to 10, review each rating. Look at the one that is rated the highest. Determine if this is really the solution that you would like to pick. If so, use the other skills you have learned in this treatment program (problem-solving, organizing, to-do list, calendar book) to implement it.

Problem-Solving Form: Selection of Action Plan

Statement of the problem: _____

_____

_____

Instructions for form:

1. List all of the possible solutions that you can think of. List them even if you think they don't make sense or you don't think you would do them. The point is to come up with AS MANY solutions AS POSSIBLE.
2. List the pros and cons of each solution.
3. After listing the pros and cons of each, give a rating, review the whole list, and give a rating to each solution.
4. Use additional copies of this sheet as needed (even if it's for the same problem).

Possible Solution	Pros of Solution	Cons of Solution	Overall Rating of Solution (1–10)

Skill: Breaking Large Tasks Down into Manageable Steps

If a task seems overwhelming, we are much more likely to procrastinate and not even attempt to start working on the task. Even if the solution is clear, it may just feel easier to put off working on the overwhelming task. By learning how to break large tasks down into smaller, more manageable steps, you will increase the likelihood that you will *start* (and therefore eventually complete) important tasks.

Steps in Breaking Large Tasks Down into Manageable Steps

1. **Choose a difficult or complex task from your to-do list** (or the "solution plan" from the previous exercise).

2. **List the steps that you must complete.**

    You can do this using small note cards or plain paper. Ask questions such as, "What is the first thing that you would need to do to make this happen?"

3. **For each step, make sure that it is manageable.**

    Ask yourself, "Is this something that you could realistically complete in one day?" and "Is this something that I would want to put off doing?" If the step itself is overwhelming, then break that step into steps. Don't be afraid to have more steps.

4. **List each individual step on your daily to-do list.**

Potential Pitfalls

You may find that distractibility interferes with your ability to use these skills. Don't despair! You will learn skills for coping with distractibility in the next module. It is important to focus on one set of skills at a time so that you can make progress. Try to focus on applying the organizational skills as best you can, and don't worry about the issues that you have not learned to deal with yet.

Also, you may find that you have some difficulty figuring out how to rate the pros, cons, and overall desirability of solutions—deciding how many steps make sense for each task. Remember, each new skill will take lots of practice before it comes naturally to you. The most important thing is that you are trying to learn new skills so that you can be more effective and organized. Just keep trying! It will get easier as you get used to using the new skills.

Homework

✎ Use your calendar and notebook every day to make a to-do list for the day.

✎ Rate each task "A," "B," or "C."

✎ Practice doing all of the "A" tasks before the "B" tasks and all of the "B" tasks before the "C" tasks.

✎ Carry over tasks that are not completed to the next day's to-do list.

✎ Practice using the problem-solving worksheet for at least one item on your to-do list.

✎ Practice breaking down one large task from your to-do list into smaller steps.

✎ Consider any difficulties that you anticipate may interfere with your completing your homework.

Chapter 7 *Organizing Papers*

The main goal of this session is for you to learn strategies for developing an organizational system to use to deal with mail and incoming papers.

You will learn both how to "triage" (order the importance of and organize) papers as they come in and how to develop a filing system so that you can find important papers later when you need them. In addition, part of this session involves reviewing the organizational skills that you have learned in this module so that you will be ready to move on to the module on distractibility next week.

Goals

■ To continue to monitor your progress

■ To review your use of the calendar and task list

■ To review your use of the "A," "B," and "C" priority ratings

■ To review your use of problem-solving and your ability to break large tasks into manageable steps

■ To develop a sorting system for dealing with papers and mail

■ To develop a filing system for important papers

■ To identify exercises for home practice and anticipate difficulties using these techniques

Review of Symptom Severity Scale

As you have been doing each week, you should complete the ADHD self-report symptom checklist. Be sure to review your score and take note of symptoms that have improved and those that are still problematic.

Score:_____

Date:_____

Review of Medication Adherence

As you have been doing each week, you should record your prescribed dosage of medication and indicate the number of doses you missed. List triggers for missed doses.

Prescribed doses per week: _____

Doses missed this week: _____

Triggers for missed doses: _____

_____

_____

Review of Previous Modules

Each week you should review your progress implementing skills from each of the previous modules. It is important to acknowledge the successes you have achieved and to problem-solve around any difficulties.

Review: Tools for Organization and Planning

- **Calendar for managing appointments**: At this point, you should discuss any problems that you are having with using your calendar system.
- **Notebook for recording a to-do list**: Review any difficulties that you are having with writing down and using your to-do list on a daily basis.

- **Use of the "A," "B," and "C" priority ratings:** If you are having any trouble with prioritizing tasks, they should be discussed at this point.
- **Use of problem-solving (selecting an action plan) and breaking down large tasks into small steps:** Consider your use of these strategies, and practice one or both skills using examples from your current task list.

Skill: Developing a Sorting System for Mail

Most people find it somewhat difficult to organize mail, important papers, and bills. However, people with ADHD can find it overwhelming. This can lead to arguments with people you live with, failure to pay bills on time, and the misplacing of important documents.

Putting a structured system in place can make this issue feel less overwhelming and more manageable.

Using these strategies may feel unfamiliar and may take some additional time in the short term, but, in the long term, they will make organization much easier.

When you have an organizational system in place, it will decrease difficulties related to poor organization such as feeling overwhelmed or out of control, paying late fees, and missing out on opportunities because of missed deadlines or lost paperwork.

We recommend that you involve your spouse, partner, or roommate in helping come up with a system that is mutually agreeable. Here are some proposed steps.

1. Identify a central location for your triage center: This is where you will open and sort all incoming mail, bills, and paperwork. You can use a wicker basket, file tray, drawer, bowl, or a box for this purpose.

   Your central location will be _____

2. Figure out "rules" regarding keeping mail, bills, and paperwork (e.g., I will save all bills for 6 months).

   _____

   _____

   _____

   _____

   _____

3. Gather all necessary items to keep with triage center: You should keep your checkbook, stamps, pens, calculator, address book, and other supplies nearby so that you don't need to go searching for them when you need to pay a bill or respond to a letter. And once you place these items in the triage center—use them there and only there!

4. Choose two or three times per week when you will go through the items in the triage center and take any action that is required (pay bill, make phone call, respond to letter). Use your calendar book and task list to help with planning this.

5. Write your "triage times" in your calendar. Problem-solve to make sure that you are not choosing times when it is unrealistic to think that you will have enough time to deal with all of the items or when you will be too tired or stressed to be effective at this task.

6. If you experience negative thoughts and you want to give up, try not to give in to this impulse. You will learn how to cope with negative thoughts in the upcoming module on adaptive thinking.

Note regarding paying bills: One big concern that we frequently hear about from individuals with ADHD is the issue of not wanting to pay the bill until near the time it is due. Some people feel that this will save money because if they do this for all of their bills, they will get more interest in the money in the bank. Other people feel that they want to wait because they just simply want to have their money longer. Others just simply procrastinate paying bills. Typically, what happens is that people who try this end up paying bills late, incurring fees, and losing money.

The best time to deal with bills and other household to-do items is right away. We suggest that you go through the triage system three times a week because many individuals do not like doing it. However, sometimes it is just as easy to pay the bill right away as it is to file the bill for payment later. Using the OHIO (Only Handle It Once) technique can save you lots of time, money, and aggravation.

SKILL: Developing a Filing System

We recommend a system that is both simple yet effective. Some people try to have a complicated system of filing, with many subfiles, subfolders, and so on. This becomes difficult to use, takes too much time, and leads people to abandon the system.

The filing system should be used for THE MOST IMPORTANT ITEMS ONLY. We recommend that you throw away anything that you do not critically need. Your spouse or partner can help you decide what is best for this. Many individuals with ADHD tend to "hoard" items, thinking that they may be needed later.

Organizational rule: Items such as newspapers and old magazines should rarely be kept, if ever.

1. Decide where you will keep your filing system. *(Don't spend too much time making this decision.)*

2. Pick one or two file drawers or a small filing cabinet to use. Keep it simple! You need to keep only things that you will *really need.*

3. Buy hanging file folders for main categories and smaller folders for subcategories.

4. Set up your main files (automobile, medical information, taxes, bank statements, credit card statements).

5. Set up your subcategories (e.g., in credit card file, you could have subfiles for Mastercard, Visa, American Express, and so on). Try to keep the system simple. As the system becomes more complicated, the likelihood that you will use it is reduced.

6. Plan specific times each week that you will use the filing system. Problem-solve to make sure that you are not choosing unrealistic times.

7. Remember that it is important to practice these skills for long enough that they become a habit. Don't give up too soon!

Thinking that everything is important. This is just not true. Discuss with people who are close to you what is and what is not important and come up with a firm list.

It may take some time in the short term to set up these systems, but it will be worth it in the long term. Try to use the strategies of problem-solving and breaking down large tasks into smaller steps if you feel overwhelmed by the prospect of setting up the triage and filing systems. If you take one step at a time, you will be able to complete these tasks.

You may need to discuss the triage and filing systems with other family members before you set them up. It will work much better if everyone is "on the same page" about where everything goes (if your spouse is still putting the mail in a big pile on the chair and you are trying to use the triage system, it won't work very well).

HOMEWORK

- Use your notebook every day to review your active to-do list.

- Rate each task as "A," "B," or "C."

- Practice doing all of the "A" tasks before the "B" tasks and all of the "B" tasks before the "C" tasks.

- Use problem-solving skills (selection of action plan, breaking down tasks into steps as needed).

- Start using your triage center to sort bills, papers, and mail. Involve people who are close to you with this as necessary.

- Start filing important papers in your filing system.

Reducing Distractibility

Chapter 8

Gauging Your Attention Span and Distractibility Delay

The main goals of this session are for you to (1) figure out how long you can maintain your attention when doing "dreaded" tasks, and (2) start implementing the "distractibility delay."

The distractibility delay involves timing your ability to stay focused on difficult activities and reducing tasks into "chunks" that take approximately that length of time. You will also learn how to delay the time when you become distracted from the task at hand.

Goals

- To continue to monitor your progress

- To review your use of the calendar, task list, and work from previous modules

- To learn how to gauge your attention span and develop a plan for breaking tasks down into steps that take that length of time

- To implement the distractibility delay

- To identify exercises for home practice and anticipate difficulties using these techniques

Review of Symptom Severity Scale

As you have been doing each week, you should complete the ADHD self-report symptom checklist. Be sure to review your score and take note of symptoms that have improved and those that are still problematic.

Score: _____

Date: _____

Review of Medication Adherence

As you have been doing each week, you should record your prescribed dosage of medication and indicate the number of doses you missed. List triggers for missed doses.

Prescribed doses per week: _____

Doses missed this week: _____

Triggers for missed doses: _____

_____

_____

Review of Previous Modules

Each week you should review your progress implementing skills from each of the previous modules. It is important to acknowledge the successes you have achieved and to problem-solve around any difficulties.

Review: Tools for Organization and Planning

- **Calendar for managing appointments**: At this point, you should discuss any problems that you are having with using your calendar system.

- **Notebook for recording a to-do list**: Review any difficulties that you are having with writing down and using your to-do list on a daily basis.

- **Use of the "A," "B," and "C" priority ratings**: If you are having any trouble with prioritizing tasks, they should be discussed at this point.

- **Use of problem-solving (selecting an action plan) and breaking down large tasks into small steps**: Consider your use of these strategies and practice one or both skills using examples from your current task list.

Patients with ADHD commonly report that they are unable to complete tasks because other less important tasks or distractions get in the way. Having a short attention span is part of ADHD. We do not view having a short attention span as being associated with a lack of intelligence or ability but rather as suggesting that people with ADHD need to use extra skills in order to cope.

There are many examples of people who can do extraordinary things despite having certain limitations. An extreme example is the musician Stevie Wonder. He used extra coping skills in order to become a top recording star, despite the fact that he is blind.

The goal of treatment is to help you function at an optimal level. We will use several strategies to help you accomplish this goal.

Gauging Your Attention Span

1. First, estimate the length of time that you can work on a boring or unattractive task without stopping.

2. Next, use the problem-solving skills that you learned earlier to break down a task into steps that last this length of time. For example, if you think that you can work on a boring task for 10 minutes, break down a larger task (e.g., paying bills) into 10-minute chunks.

▓ *TIME IT!* ▓

During the upcoming week, pick a task you know you have been avoiding.

Find a stopwatch. We recommend that you purchase a wristwatch that includes multiple alarm times, as well as a stopwatch and a timer. For these exercises, you can also use a kitchen timer or other type of timer that will allow you to keep track of how long you can sustain your attention on a single task.

▓ Figure out a time when you can work on a task that you may find boring or difficult or that you have been avoiding.

- Get out the stopwatch (or use a clock, recording the start and end time).

- Begin working.

- Keep going as long as you normally would before either taking a break, going to the bathroom, or allowing a strong distraction to pop into your head.

- When the urge comes to stop working, hit the stopwatch and see how long you were able to stick with the task (or record the time).

Repeat this exercise a couple of times. Average the amount of time that passed before you became distracted, and make this your starting attention span time.

The trick is to use the problem-solving skills you learned earlier to break down overwhelming or boring tasks into chunks that take approximately the amount of time that you can maintain your attention. We recommend taking breaks only between the chunks.

As you do this more and more, you can try to increase the length of your attention span, also using the skill described in the next section.

Skill: Distractibility Delay

When you are working on a boring task, it is inevitable that distractions will pop into your head from time to time and serve as big temptations. Many times the distractions appear to grow in terms of how important they seem to be.

The difficult problem here is this: Is it really that these distractions are important or is it that they become more important because

1. They are not the task you had set out to do.

2. The task you set out to do is now not attractive.

Is it important or just more attractive? A good example came from one of our patients who was working on his master's thesis. He told us that whenever he sat down to do his work, he would feel the need to clean his apartment. He did not like cleaning but would have the urge to clean whenever he needed to write. In fact, he got to the point where he felt that he just could not work unless everything in his apartment was cleaned and in order! Over the years, we have found that other patients who were in school reported similar stories. We now believe that the cleanest apartments in the world belong to graduate students who need to do their theses! In these cases, cleaning becomes a distraction that grows in importance. Even though it is typically not an attractive or important task, it becomes much more attractive than the task at hand, which feels overwhelming.

The distractibility delay is an exercise that can be done in addition to what we described earlier. The distractibility delay technique was inspired by a similar technique used in treatment of generalized anxiety disorder, articulated by Craske, Barlow, and O'Leary (1992).

Once you have determined the length of time you can maintain your attention and you have broken down tasks into steps that take about that amount of time, we recommend that you try to build skills in delaying distractions when you are working.

Steps for Distractibility Delay

1. Put your notebook next to you.

2. Set your timer for a specific length of time, either the length of time you can usually maintain your attention or, if you are trying to build this up, for *slightly* longer.

3. Start working on a task.

4. When a distraction pops into your head, write it down in your notebook but don't do anything about it (e.g., don't get up and start making a phone call, putting something away, writing a check, and so on).

5. Once the distraction has been written down, you can use coping statements such as "I will worry about it later," "This is not an A-priority task," or "I will come back to this."

6. Return to the original task until you are finished with the chunk of work that you have selected.

7. When the timer goes off, take a break. At this point, you can look at your distraction list and decide if you want to deal with them now or later.

8. When done working for the day, go back to the distraction list. Decide if these are actually important or if they are things that became attractive only because they were not the task you were working on.

9. If they are in fact important, either do them or add them to your task list.

Potential Pitfalls

These skills may seem simple, but they aren't! Don't expect yourself to be able to use them effectively right away. The extra coping skills that you are learning to help you overcome your short attention span and distractibility may take some time to develop. Remember, it took you many years to develop your current habits, and it will take some time to develop these more effective habits. Stick with this program; it will be worth it in the long run!

✎ Start using problem-solving to break down boring tasks into chunks that fit the length of your attention span.

✎ Use the distractibility delay technique when you are working on aversive or boring tasks.

✎ Use your notebook every day to review your active to-do list.

✎ Rate each task as "A," "B," or "C."

✎ Practice doing all of the "A" tasks before the "B" tasks and all of the "B" tasks before the "C" tasks.

✎ Use problem-solving skills (selection of action plan, breaking down tasks into steps as needed).

✎ Keep up with using your triage center to sort bills, papers, and mail. Involve people who are close to you with this as necessary.

✎ Keep up with filing important papers in your filing system.

Chapter 9   *Modifying Your Environment*

The main goals of this session are for you to learn how to modify your environment to reduce distractibility and for you to learn how to create "reminders" for you to focus on the task at hand.

You will learn how to reduce the number of distractions in your environment and create a situation that is more conducive to concentration. You will also learn several strategies that will help you check in with yourself to see if you are distracted. This will enable you to refocus your attention on the task at hand if you have become distracted.

Goals

- To continue to monitor your progress

- To review your continual use of skills from previous modules

- To continue breaking tasks down into steps that match the duration of your attention span and using the distractibility delay

- To learn how to reduce the number of things that are likely to distract you in your environment

- To learn how to check in with yourself to see if you are distracted and learn how to refocus on the task at hand when you do become distracted

- To identify exercises for home practice and anticipate difficulties using these techniques

Review of Symptom Severity Scale

As you have been doing each week, you should complete the ADHD self-report symptom checklist. Be sure to review your score and take note of symptoms that have improved and those that are still problematic.

Score:_____

Date:_____

Review of Medication Adherence

As you have been doing each week, you should record your prescribed dosage of medication and indicate the number of doses you missed. List triggers for missed doses.

Prescribed doses per week: _____

Doses missed this week: _____

Triggers for missed doses: _____

_____

_____

Review of Previous Modules

Each week you should review your progress implementing skills from each of the previous modules. It is important to acknowledge the successes you have achieved and to problem-solve around any difficulties.

Review: Tools for Organization and Planning

■ **Calendar for managing appointments:** At this point, you should discuss any problems that you are having with using your calendar system.

- **Notebook for recording a to-do list:** Review any difficulties that you are having with writing down and using your to-do list on a daily basis.

- **Use of the "A," "B," and "C" priority ratings:** If you are having any trouble with prioritizing tasks, they should be discussed at this point.

- **Use of problem-solving (selecting an action plan) and breaking down large tasks into small steps:** Consider your use of these strategies, and practice one or both skills using examples from your current task list.

Review: Tools for Reducing Distractibility

- **Breaking tasks down into manageable chunks:** At this point, you should discuss with your therapist any problems that you are having with breaking down tasks.

- **Use of the distractibility delay:** Review any difficulties that you are having with the distractibility delay technique.

Skill: Controlling Your Work Environment

It is important for individuals with ADHD to work in an environment that has few distractions. Even with the coping with distractibility skills already discussed, most people are somewhat distractible when they are trying to concentrate. Sometimes, distractions interfere to the point that it becomes impossible to get things done.

At this time, think about the environment in which you try to do work, schoolwork, or important household tasks (e.g., paying bills). Ask yourself, "What are the things that typically distract me from my work?"

Some typical distractions include:

- hearing the telephone ring

- surfing the Internet, chatting on line, playing on-line games

- replying to e-mails or instant messages

- noticing other things on the desk or table that need attention

- listening to something on the radio

- watching something on the television

- speaking to a friend or relative who is in the room

- looking at something going on outside the window

What are the types of things that typically get in the way when you are trying to get a project done? For each item that is distracting to you, you should come up with a strategy that reduces your susceptibility to this distraction.

For example, you can:

- turn off the phone

- close your Web browser and/or e-mail

- shut off the noise that beeps when you receive a new e-mail message

- clear off your desk or workspace

- turn off the radio and television

- ask others not to disturb you because you are working

- turn your desk away from the window

Use the table on the following page to identify and eliminate usual distractions for your work environment.

Strategies for Reducing Distractions

Distraction	Environmental Reduction Strategy

Location, location, location! We recommend finding one place in your home where you can do important tasks without distraction. This place should be a place that you can focus on to keep clear. It could be your desk, a table near your desk, or any other "work space." Many people report that their desk becomes cluttered. It is certainly difficult to keep a desk clean. Of course, you can use your filing system. However, if you think that you may not be able to keep your desk clear, find another space that you can use that you will keep clear, and make this your work space.

One hallmark of ADHD is that that people with this disorder frequently lose important items. This is problematic because it can cause lateness and increase feelings of frustration.

At this point, take a moment to think of any difficulties that you experience with keeping track of important objects, such as your keys, wallet, notebook, appointment book, or Palm Pilot. Some of these may be objects that you need to take with you whenever you leave the house.

The next step is to think of a specific place where you will keep these objects. Some people place a basket somewhere near the door and place the important objects in the basket each time that they come in the door. Others have a hanging rack for all keys. You may be able to place all of your important objects in one place, or you may need to come up with several different places.

By having specific places where the important objects belong, you are more likely to be able to locate the objects when you need them. But you need to work to develop the habit; the goal is to never put down your keys or other valued object in any location except the target location. Never!

You can improve the success of this technique by involving other family members in the process. You can tell everyone in the household where things belong and ask them to either put the items away or remind you to do so if they notice that something is out of place (of course, you have to agree to not get mad at them when they remind you!).

The other important (and many times difficult) task to do is this: whenever you see one of these object out of place, immediately return it to the specified site.

Skill: Using Reminders

Imagine that you could have someone follow you around and constantly remind you about all of the skills that we have discussed. Having this person around would greatly increase your use of the skills. You would never forget. So many of these skills require actively remembering to do them (although, with practice, these become habits, and you eventually won't have to actively remember).

For most people, a 24-hour personal assistant is not feasible. We therefore recommend a low-cost reminder device: sticker dots. These have proved to be very helpful to people who need a visible reminder. You can place these dots on items that typically distract you, such as the telephone, the computer, the radio, the window, or the refrigerator. You should place them where they will be visible to you.

Each time that you see an adhesive dot, you should ask yourself the following questions: "Am I doing what I am supposed to be doing, or did I get distracted?" and "Am I remembering to use my skills for ADHD?" If you notice that you have become distracted, you should return to the task at hand immediately.

Skill: Using an Alarm Device

An alarm device can be helpful in getting you to check in with yourself on a regular basis about whether or not you are on task. You can use an alarm clock, an alarm on your watch, a Palm Pilot, a computer, or a cell phone.

You should set the alarm to go off at regularly scheduled intervals. Many watches have a feature that allow it to go off each hour. We, however, recommend trying to have the device sound each half-hour, especially when you are trying to be productive.

When the alarm sounds, ask yourself, "Am I doing what I am supposed to be doing, or did I get distracted?" As we discussed earlier, if you notice that you have become distracted, immediately return to the task at hand.

It is easy to get frustrated with these strategies if they don't work right away. Remember, you are trying to develop new work habits. It takes lots of practice before new habits become second nature. Don't give up. Even if it seems like these skills don't work at first, keep at them. It will pay off in the long run when you will be less susceptible to distractions and get more accomplished.

Homework

✎ Use your notebook every day to review your active to-do list.

✎ Rate each task as "A," "B," or "C."

✎ Practice doing all of the "A" tasks before the "B" tasks and all of the "B" tasks before the "C" tasks.

✎ Use problem-solving skills (selection of action plan, breaking down tasks into steps as needed).

✎ Use your triage center to sort bills, papers, and mail. Involve people who are close to you with this as necessary.

✎ File important papers in your filing system.

✎ Use problem-solving skills to break down boring tasks into chunks that fit the length of your attention span.

✎ Use the distractibility delay technique when you are working on aversive or boring tasks.

✎ Use your skills to reduce distractions in your work environment.

✎ Start putting important objects in specific places.

✎ Use colored dots as reminders to check in with yourself to see if you have become distracted.

✎ Use your alarm to check in with yourself to see if you have become distracted.

Adaptive Thinking

Chapter 10   *Introduction to a Cognitive Model of ADHD*

By now, you have developed systems for organizing, planning, and problem-solving and have been practicing skills for managing distractibility. The next section, targeting adaptive thinking, will help you increase your awareness of negative thoughts that can cause stress, cause mood problems, and interfere with the successful completion of tasks.

This method of training yourself to think adaptively has been used in similar cognitive-behavioral treatments and has been effective in treating many other psychological disorders such as depression and anxiety disorders.[1] The major goal of learning to think about tasks and situations adaptively is to reduce the times when negative thoughts or moods interfere with tasks, follow-through, distress, or add to distractibility

Adaptive thinking will enable you to:

- Increase your awareness of negative, interfering thoughts

- Develop strategies for keeping your thoughts in check

- Minimize symptoms

Goals

- To continue to monitor your progress

- To review homework from previous modules

- To learn basic principles of the cognitive model of mood

- To become skilled in identifying and labeling unhelpful automatic thoughts

- To identify exercises for home practice

---

[1] This method of implementing and teaching cognitive-restructuring skills is based on McDermott (2000), as well as other CBT therapy manuals, including Hope et al.'s (2000) manual for the treatment of social phobia and the Otto et al. (1996) manual for treatment of panic disorder in the context of medication discontinuation.

Review of Symptom Severity Scale

As you have been doing each week, you should complete the ADHD self-report symptom checklist. Be sure to review your score and take note of symptoms that have improved and those that are still problematic.

Score:_____

Date:_____

Review of Medication Adherence

As you have been doing each week, you should record your prescribed dosage of medication and indicate the number of doses you missed. List triggers for missed doses.

Prescribed doses per week: _____

Doses missed this week: _____

Triggers for missed doses: _____

Review of Previous Modules

Each week you should review your progress implementing skills from each of the previous modules. It is important to acknowledge the successes you have achieved and to problem-solve around any difficulties.

Review: Tools for Organization and Planning

- Calendar for managing appointments

- Notebook for recording a to-do list

- Notebook for breaking tasks down into subtasks

- Notebook for managing and prioritizing multiple tasks

- Strategies for problem-solving and developing an action plan

- Triage and filing systems

Review: Strategies for Managing Distractibility

- Breaking tasks down to correspond to duration of attention span and taking breaks between tasks

- Utilizing distractibility delay

- Using stimulus control for environment (removing distractions)

- Using stimulus control for important objects (identifying specific place for each)

- Distractibility reminders (dots and alarm): "Am I doing what I am supposed to be doing?"

The Cognitive-Behavioral Model

Adaptive thinking is important because of the interrelationship among thoughts, feelings, and behaviors.

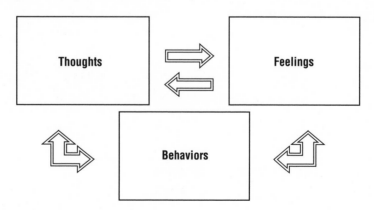

This model emphasizes the important connections among your thoughts, feelings, and behaviors in a given situation. The cognitive part of cognitive-behavioral therapy involves the way in which thoughts contribute to how people act and thoughts contribute to how people feel.

In the course of a given day, numerous thoughts go through your mind. What is surprising is that often you are not particularly aware of these thoughts. However, they play an important role in determining how you are feeling in a situation and how you may respond. When you are feeling overwhelmed or stressed or are anticipating the completion of a task, the thoughts that go through your mind play a critical role in determining the outcome of your situation.

These thoughts are "automatic"; they happen on their own. For example, think about when you first learned to drive a car. In order to coordinate many tasks at once, you had to be conscious of handling the steering wheel, remembering to signal for turns, staying exactly in your lane, averting other traffic, and trying to park. Doing so many tasks at the same time required your total attention.

Now, think about driving today. You probably know how to drive without actively thinking about what you are doing. You likely don't even remember thinking about all of these steps because they have become automatic.

Less Helpful Automatic Thinking

In many situations, automatic thoughts enable us to complete a task more easily. Unfortunately, in other situations, automatic thoughts interfere with achieving goals. For example, imagine you have to do task you will probably not enjoy, such as preparing your tax return. Imagine the following types of thoughts going through your mind:

"I am careless and am going to do this wrong."

"This is going to take forever."

"If I complete my return, I will realize I owe money."

"If I owe money I am going to not have enough for rent."

If these thoughts are going through your head, then you can easily see that this task will feel overwhelming and stressful. This will increase the chances that you will procrastinate by doing any other possible task.

The behavioral component here is usually some form of avoidance. Negative thoughts about a situation make a person avoid the situation because they (1) feel worse and (2) expect the outcome of the situation to be negative. Avoidance can lead to more anxiety, restlessness, and perhaps irritability or depression; the task doesn't get done, and the person feels even worse about it.

Anxiety and depression may lead to more negative thinking, and around and around the cycle goes, making the problem worse and worse.

For people with ADHD, this cycle worsens other symptoms such as inattention, procrastination, frustration, and depression.

The first step in breaking this cycle is to identify and slow down negative, automatic thinking. Becoming more aware of situations when this occurs is the first step in learning to think in more adaptive ways.

Skill: Identifying Negative Automatic Thoughts

The Thought Record is a tool that was developed to help you learn how to identify, slow down, and restructure negative automatic thoughts. You can use the worksheets provided or even use your notebook by drawing in the columns and headings.

Let's start with a distressing situation you experienced in the past week. Think about the past week and see if you can identify a time when you felt overwhelmed, stressed, sad, or upset.

This worksheet is best done with the aid of your therapist and takes a good amount of time to learn how to do. We recommend practicing it over several sessions.

Column 1 should contain a brief description of the **situation**. When did it take place, where were you, with whom, what was going on, and so on? Ideally, the description of the situation will be a sentence or two at most.

Column 2 should have your **thoughts**. What was going through your mind at the time? What were you saying to yourself about the situation, other people, and your role in the situation? What are you afraid might happen? What is the worst thing that could have happened if this feared outcome had occurred? What does this mean about how the other person feels/thinks about you?

When coming up with automatic thoughts, it is important to separate thoughts from feelings. Thoughts are what you think of the situation. Feelings go in the next column.

Column 3 should be a list of the **mood** or emotions you experienced (you may list several different feelings). Rate the **intensity** of each feeling on a scale of 0–100

(0 = the least intense, 100 = the most intense). Examples of moods include angry, upset, happy, sad, depressed, anxious, surprised.

Time and Situation	Automatic Thoughts	Mood and Intensity
At home, thinking about doing my taxes	This is going to be so much work. I am never going to finish it. I am never going to find everything I need to. I am going to get audited. I am going to end up having to pay so much money.	Overwhelmed (80) Anxious (75) Frustrated (80)

Form: Three-Column Thought Record

Time and Situation	Automatic Thoughts	Mood and Intensity

Introduction to Thinking Errors

Now that you see how certain situations can trigger automatic thoughts and subsequent negative (or, at times, positive) feelings, let's look more closely at the nature of these automatic thoughts. In our experience, and in the work of other cognitive-behavioral therapists, common types of negative automatic thoughts often emerge. Moreover, we can begin to see how these types of thoughts may interfere with your ability to complete tasks and also contribute to feeling depressed, anxious, or frustrated.

What follows is a list of common thinking errors. This list is taken from Hope, Heimberg, Juster, and Turk (2000), with some modifications. The list from Hope et al. (2000) was in turn based on Persons (1989). You should review each error to make sure you understand them all and to begin to look for patterns and determine which types of errors may be especially problematic for you.

All-or-nothing thinking: You see things in black and white categories—for example, ALL aspects of a project need to be completed immediately, or, if your performance falls short of perfect, you see it as a total failure.

Overgeneralization: You see a single negative event as part of a never-ending pattern.

Mental filter: You pick out a single negative detail and dwell on it exclusively, over-looking other positive aspects of the situation.

Disqualifying the positive: You reject positive experiences by insisting they "don't count" for some reason or other. In this way, you can maintain a negative belief that is contradicted by your everyday experiences.

Jumping to conclusions: You make a negative interpretation even though there are no facts that convincingly support your conclusion.

> *Mind reading:* You arbitrarily conclude that someone is reacting negatively to you, and you don't bother to check this out.

> *Fortune telling:* You anticipate that things will turn out badly, and you feel that your prediction is a predetermined fact.

Magnification/minimization: You exaggerate the importance of things (such as your mistake, or someone else's achievement), or you inappropriately shrink things until they appear tiny (your own desirable qualities or the other's imperfections).

Catastrophizing: You attribute extreme and horrible consequences to the outcomes of events. One mistake at work is the same as being fired from your job.

Emotional reasoning: You assume that your negative emotions necessarily reflect the way things really are: "I feel it, so it must be true."

"Should" statements: You try to motivate yourself with "shoulds" and "shouldn'ts" as if you need to be punished before you can be expected to do anything. With regard to others, you feel anger, frustration, and resentment.

Labeling and mislabeling: This is an extreme form of overgeneralization. Instead of describing an error, you attach a negative label to yourself or others.

Personalization: You see negative events as indicative of some negative characteristic of yourself or others, or you take responsibility for events that were not your doing.

Maladaptive thinking: You focus on a thought that may be true but over which you have no control. Excessively focusing on one thought can be a form of self-criticism and can distract you from an important task or from attempting new behaviors.

Now that you have learned about common types of thinking errors, let's go back to the Thought Record you filled out earlier. For each of the automatic thoughts you listed, review the list of thinking errors and see if you can identify these common patterns in your thinking. Then, list the appropriate thinking error in **Column 4** of the table.

Keep in mind that not all negative thoughts represent thinking errors. Sometimes it is realistic for a situation to produce a negative thought, which in turn contributes to a negative feeling. For example, imagine you had studied for an exam for many days and you were driving to school to take the exam. Then, suddenly you encountered a traffic jam caused by a car accident that occurred earlier. Now, if your thought was "Oh no, I hope I won't be late. I studied so hard for this exam," and you were feeling anxious and perhaps frustrated, that would make sense! The challenge for you would be to *problem-solve*—to try to stay calm, perhaps call the instructor to let her know that you were going to be late, and to focus on driving safely.

However, if in addition to those thoughts you also said to yourself, "Bad things always happen to me, I can never do anything right, I am going to miss the exam and fail the class," we can imagine that your anxiety and despair would intensify, and you might be more likely to drive dangerously. Furthermore, if you did get to the exam in time, you most likely would not be able to concentrate as well as you had when you were studying. Looking closely, you can see that these thoughts, respectively, could be classified as *overgeneralization, personalization*, and *jumping to conclusions*. See the following example; then use the chart to record your own.

Example: Four-Column Thought Record

Time and Situation	Automatic Thoughts	Mood and Intensity	Thinking Error
Preparing a report for work	I have to do all of this today.	Overwhelmed (80)	All-or-nothing thinking
	I must do this perfectly.	Anxious (75)	All-or-nothing thinking
	If I do not finish my boss will be upset.	Depressed (60)	Jumping to conclusions (mind reading)
	If the project is not perfect and my boss is upset, I will lose my job.		Jumping to conclusions (fortune telling), catastrophizing

Form: Four-Column Thought Record

Time and Situation	Automatic Thoughts	Mood and Intensity	Thinking Error

Potential Pitfalls

For some people, writing out negative thoughts makes the thoughts "seem more real" or more difficult to cope with. Because of this, they are reluctant to utilize Thought Records. However, the thought is in your mind, interfering, regardless of whether you write it down. Completing the Thought Record will actually help you feel better about the situation, despite the initial difficulty of seeing your thought on paper.

You may find that it is hard to label your feeling(s) and may think that you have to come up with the perfect emotion to describe your feelings. In actuality, this is not true. Use the first word that comes to mind, even if it is not perfect. Over time, it will become easier to label your feelings.

Homework

As you have learned from the previous modules, practicing new skills is vital so that you become familiar with them, are able to easily use the tools, and begin to see the positive results that can emerge when you consistently use these CBT strategies. Recognize that at first, when you are learning a new skill, it may feel awkward, may be confusing, and may require effort to implement. That's okay! The more you practice, the easier it will become.

For this week:

- Continue utilizing and reviewing skills from previous modules.

- Read the form Preliminary Instructions for Adaptive Thinking.

- Complete Thought Records for at least two situations during the week.

In this session, try to anticipate which situations you may want to work on in the upcoming week. In addition, be sure to anticipate any problems that may get in the way of completing the homework. For example, having a busy schedule, going out of town, or being uncertain about how to complete an assignment may make it more difficult to practice your skills. We have found that if you can anticipate and problem-solve in advance, these obstacles can become manageable, and you will be more likely to achieve success with the new skills.

Remember that you do not have to complete these home assignments perfectly! The idea is to begin monitoring your thoughts that arise in difficult situations and to begin practicing identifying the common types of thinking errors.

The purpose of the Thought Records is to identify automatic thoughts in situations that lead to feeling overwhelmed.

The first step in learning to think in more useful ways is to become more aware of these thoughts and their relationship to your mood. If you are anticipating a stressful situation or a task that is making you feel overwhelmed, write out your thoughts regarding this situation.

If a situation has already passed and you find that you are thinking about it negatively, list your thoughts for this situation.

The **first column** is a description of the situation.

The **second column** is for you to list your thoughts during a stressful, overwhelming, or uncontrollable situation.

The **third column** is for you to write down what emotions you are having and what you mood is like when thinking these thoughts (e.g., depressed, sad, angry).

The **fourth column** is for you to see if your thoughts match the list of "thinking errors." These may include:

- All-or-nothing thinking

- Overgeneralizations

- Jumping to conclusions: fortune telling/mind reading

- Magnification/minimization

- Emotional reasoning

- "Should" statements

- Labeling and mislabeling

- Personalization

- Maladaptive thinking

Form: Four-Column Thought Record

Time/Situation	Automatic Thoughts	Mood/Intensity	Thinking Errors

Chapter 11   *Adaptive Thinking*

Goals

■ To continue to monitor your progress with the symptom checklist

■ To review homework from previous modules

■ To review Thought Records completed at home

■ To discuss coaching styles and coaching story

■ To discuss formulation of a rational response

■ To identify exercises for home practice

Review of Symptom Severity Scale

As you have been doing each week, you should complete the ADHD self-report symptom checklist. Be sure to review your score and take note of symptoms that have improved and those that are still problematic.

Score:_____

Date:_____

Review of Medication Adherence

As you have been doing each week, you should record your prescribed dosage of medication and indicate the number of doses you missed. List triggers for missed doses.

Prescribed doses per week: _____

Doses missed this week: _____

Triggers for missed doses: _____

Review of Previous Modules

Each week you should review your progress implementing skills from each of the previous modules. It is important to acknowledge the successes you have achieved and to problem-solve around any difficulties.

Review: Tools for Organization and Planning

■ Calendar for managing appointments

■ Notebook for recording a to-do list

■ Notebook for breaking tasks down into subtasks

■ Notebook for managing and prioritizing multiple tasks

■ Strategies for problem-solving and developing an action plan

■ Triage and filing systems

Review: Strategies for Managing Distractibility

- Breaking tasks down to match duration of attention span and taking breaks between tasks

- Utilizing distractibility delay

- Using stimulus control for environment (removing distractions)

- Using stimulus control for important objects (identifying specific place for each)

- Distractibility reminders (dots and alarm): "Am I doing what I am supposed to be doing?"

Review: Adaptive Thinking

- Using the Thought Record to identify and label automatic thoughts

Homework Review

Review the Thought Records you completed at home. If you were not able to complete any Thought Records, try to identify the obstacles that may have interfered, and use the problem-solving skills to determine the best way to work on automatic thinking. Did you have difficulty making time for home practice? Were the directions confusing? Was it difficult to see your thoughts in writing?

If you didn't do any at home, it may be useful to practice doing one before going on.

If you did, then you should review each situation: the automatic thoughts and the thinking errors that you identified. Did you see any patterns?

Sometimes it can be tricky to sort out thoughts from feelings. Your therapist can help with this, and you can practice asking yourself, "Is this what I was *thinking* or *feeling?*"

In this session, you will learn strategies for correcting thinking errors and developing more helpful thoughts. Our goal is to help you transform the unhelpful, interfering thoughts into more supportive, coaching thoughts. In order to understand how powerful your thoughts can be, we like to tell a coaching story (taken from Otto, 1999).

Coaching Story

This is a story about little league baseball. I talk about little league baseball because of the amazing parents and coaches involved. And by "amazing" I don't mean good. I mean extreme.

But this story doesn't start with the coaches or the parents; it starts with Johnny, who is a little league player in the outfield. His job is to catch "fly balls" and return them to the infield players. On this particular day of our story, Johnny is in the outfield. And "crack!"—one of the players on the other team hits a fly ball. The ball is coming to Johnny. Johnny raises his glove. The ball is coming to him, it is coming to him . . . and it goes over his head. Johnny misses the ball, and the other team scores a run.

Now there are a number of ways a coach can respond to this situation. Let's take Coach A first. Coach A is the type of coach who will come out on the field and shout: "I can't believe you missed that ball! Anyone could have caught it! My dog could have caught it! You screw up like that again and you'll be sitting on the bench! That was lousy!"

Coach A then storms off the field. At this point, if Johnny is anything like I am, he is standing there, tense, tight, trying not to cry, and praying that another ball is not hit to him. If a ball does come to him, Johnny will probably miss it. After all, he is tense, tight, and he may see four balls coming to him because of the tears in his eyes. Also, if we are Johnny's parents, we may see more profound changes after the game: Johnny, who typically places his baseball glove on the mantle, now throws it under his bed. And before the next game, he may complain that his stomach hurts, that perhaps he should not go to the game. This is the scenario with Coach A.

Now let's go back to the original event and play it differently. Johnny has just missed the fly ball, and now Coach B comes out on the field. Coach B says: "Well you missed that one. Here is what I want you to remember: fly balls always look like they are farther away than they really are. Also, it is much easier to run forward than to back up. Because of this, I want you to prepare for the ball by taking a few extra steps backwards. Run forward if you need to, but try to catch it at chest level, so you can adjust your hand if you misjudge the ball. Let's see how you do next time."

Coach B leaves the field. How does Johnny feel? Well, he is not happy. After all, he missed the ball—but there are a number of important differences from the way he felt with Coach A. He is not as tense or tight, and if a fly ball does come to him, he knows what to do differently to catch it. And because he does not have tears in his eyes, he may actually see the ball accurately. He may catch the next one.

So, if we were the type of parent that eventually wants Johnny to make the major leagues, we would pick Coach B, because he teaches Johnny how to be a more effective player. Johnny knows what to do differently, may catch more balls, and may excel at the game. But if we don't care whether Johnny makes the major leagues—because baseball is a game, and one is supposed to be able to enjoy a game—then we would still pick Coach B. We pick Coach B because we care whether Johnny enjoys the game. With Coach B, Johnny knows what to do differently; he is not tight, tense, and ready to cry; he may catch a few balls; and he may enjoy the game. And he may continue to place his glove on the mantel.

Now, while we may all select Coach B for Johnny, we rarely choose the view of Coach B for the way we talk to ourselves. Think about your last mistake. Did you say, "I can't believe I did that! I am so stupid! What a jerk!" These are "Coach A" thoughts, and they have approximately the same effect on us as they do on Johnny. They make us feel tense and tight and sometimes make us feel like crying. And this style of coaching rarely makes us do better in the future. Even if you are concerned only about productivity (making the major leagues), you would still pick Coach B. And if you were concerned with enjoying life, while guiding yourself effectively for both joy and productivity, you would still pick Coach B.

Keep in mind that we are not talking about how we coach ourselves in a baseball game. We are talking about how we coach ourselves in life, and our enjoyment of life.

During the next week, I would like you to listen to see how you are coaching yourself. And if you hear Coach A, remember this story and see if you can replace Coach A with Coach B.

This story is meant to help you recognize negative, unhelpful thoughts as they pop up (Coach A thoughts) and learn to develop more supportive, rational thinking (Coach B thoughts).

Let's go back to one of the Thought Records you previously completed. Review the automatic thoughts and thinking errors that you identified. If you have not completed a Thought Record yet, you should begin a new one now. The next step is to evaluate the helpfulness of each thought. The following questions are suggested as prompts to help you objectively evaluate these thoughts.

> *What is the evidence that this thought is true?*
>
> *Is there an alternate explanation?*
>
> *What is the worst thing that can happen? Has this situation unreasonably grown in importance?*
>
> *What would a good coach say about this situation?*
>
> *Have I done what I can to control it? If I were to do anything else, would this help or hinder the situation?*
>
> *Am I worrying excessively about this?*
>
> *What would a good friend say to me about this situation? What would I say to a good friend about this situation if he were going through it?*
>
> *Why is this statement a thinking error?*

In the last column of this form, formulate a rational response. The rational response is a statement that you can say to yourself to try to feel better about the situation. Keep in mind that we are not asking you to overlook all negative aspects of your thoughts. The idea is to come up with a more balanced, objective, and helpful way of thinking about the situation.

Form: Thought Record

Time and Situation	Automatic Thoughts	Mood and Intensity	Thinking Error	Rational Response

Potential Pitfalls

We have discussed several different types of thinking errors that can contribute to negative feelings. While it is important to be familiar with the types of errors you may be making, don't get stuck trying to find the exact type of error that corresponds with your thought. Your thought may fit into more than one category, and often these categories of thinking errors overlap. Your goal is to recognize that your automatic thought might be a thinking error, to understand why this is true, and, most important, to come up with a rational response.

Identifying a rational response may be tricky at first. Refer to the suggested questions (i.e., *what would you say to a friend who said this?*). Also, keep in mind that your thoughts and feelings about the situation may not completely change immediately after identifying a rational response. However, if you repeat the responses to yourself, it will begin to replace the negative, automatic thought you initially had.

Homework

Remember, practicing your new skills will make them feel more comfortable, and you will begin to notice improvements. First, identify situations you will work on at home using the Thought Record. Also, consider any difficulties you may have completing this assignment, and problem-solve to minimize the chance that obstacles will emerge.

For this week:

✎ Continue practicing skills you have learned in previous sections.

✎ Use your Thought Record or notebook to list automatic thoughts, thinking errors, and rational responses for situations for the following week.

✎ Read the handout on completing a rational response.

✎ Complete Thought Records for at least two situations during the week.

The purpose of adaptive thinking is to help promote optimal thinking when you are feeling stressed. The steps that are involved can be achieved using the rest of the worksheet.

Throughout the week, when you are feeling stress, sad, or overwhelmed, continue to list your thoughts for each situation. If you are anticipating a stressful situation, or a task is making you feel overwhelmed, write out your thoughts regarding this situation. If a situation has already passed and you find that you are thinking about it negatively, list your thoughts for this situation.

The **first column** is a description of the situation.

The **second column** is for you to list your thoughts during a stressful, overwhelming, or uncontrollable situation.

The **third column** is for you to write down what emotions you are having and what your mood is like when thinking these thoughts (e.g. depressed, sad, angry).

The **fourth column** is for you to see if your thoughts match the list of "thinking errors." These may include:

All-or-nothing thinking	Emotional reasoning
Overgeneralizations	"Should" statements
Jumping to conclusions: Fortune telling/mind reading	Labeling and mislabeling
	Personalization
Magnification/minimization	Maladaptive thinking

In the last column, try to come up with a rational response to each thought or to the most important negative thought. The rational response is a statement that you can say to yourself to try to feel better about the situation. Questions to help come up with this rational response can include:

What is the evidence that this thought is true? Is there an alternate explanation?

What is the worst thing that can happen?

Has this situation unreasonably grown in importance?

What would a good coach say about this situation?

Have I done what I can do to control it?

If I were to do anything else, would this help or hinder the situation?

Am I worrying excessively about this?

What would a good friend say to me about this situation?

What would I say to a good friend about this situation if he were going through it?

Why is this statement a cognitive distortion?

Form: Thought Record

Time and Situation	Automatic Thoughts (what was going through your head?)	Mood and Intensity of Mood	Thinking Errors (match thoughts from list)	Rational Response

What is the evidence for the thought? Against the thought? Why is it the particular cognitive distortion? Is there an alternate explanation? What is the worst thing that could happen? What would a good friend or good coach say? What would you say to a friend in a similar situation?

Chapter 12 | *Rehearsal and Review of Adaptive Thinking Skills*

Goals

▪ To continue to monitor your progress with the symptom checklist

▪ To review homework from previous modules

▪ To review use of Thought Records to develop more adaptive thoughts

▪ To identify exercises for home practice

Review of Symptom Severity Scale

As you have been doing each week, you should complete the ADHD self-report symptom checklist. Be sure to review your score and take note of symptoms that have improved and those that are still problematic.

Score:_____

Date:_____

Review of Medication Adherence

As you have been doing each week, you should record your prescribed dosage of medication and indicate the number of doses you missed. List triggers for missed doses.

Prescribed doses per week: _____

Doses missed this week: _____

Triggers for missed doses: _____

_____

_____

Review of Previous Modules

Each week you should check review your progress implementing skills from each of the previous modules. It is important to acknowledge the successes you have achieved and to problem-solve around any difficulties.

Review: Tools for Organization and Planning

- Calendar for managing appointments

- Notebook for recording a to-do list

- Notebook for breaking tasks down into subtasks

- Notebook for managing and prioritizing multiple tasks

- Strategies for problem-solving and developing an action plan

- Triage and filing systems

Review: Strategies for Managing Distractibility

- Breaking tasks down to match duration of attention span and taking breaks between tasks

- Utilizing distractibility delay

- Using stimulus control for environment (removing distractions)

- Using stimulus control for important objects (identifying specific place for each)

- Distractibility reminders (dots and alarm): "Am I doing what I am supposed to be doing?"

Review: Strategies for Developing Adaptive Thinking

■ Using the Thought Record to identify and label automatic thoughts

■ Identifying a rational response

Homework Review

In this session you will have a chance to review your home practice and discuss any difficulties you may be having with adaptive thinking. If necessary, complete a new Thought Record to review these skills.

Review: Adaptive Thinking

At this point, you may want to discuss and think about any new situations that may require adaptive thinking. Remember to refer to your handouts on adaptive thinking if you find you are getting stuck. Thought Records are a tool that you can easily use on your own. Initially, it is helpful to write out the four columns and walk yourself through the Thought Record. Ultimately, however, this process will take place in your mind. With practice, you will learn to spot unhelpful automatic thoughts as they emerge, and you will be able to come up with a rational response to help you feel better about the situation. When necessary, you can always write out the Thought Record and review the handouts.

We suggest using this session to review an additional situation and completing a cognitive restructuring sheet in full for this situation.

Planning for Future Parts of Treatment

Congratulations!! You have now completed the core elements of cognitive-behavioral therapy for ADHD. You should review your "goal list" that was completed at the beginning of your treatment to determine whether to do one of the optional modules or whether to do more review work on modules you have already completed.

We include one optional chapter on procrastination. The skills you have already learned can be specifically applied to the area of procrastination. It is up to you to figure out if you feel you need the extra work or if it makes more sense to review material already covered in this workbook.

Potential Pitfalls

You have done a lot of work to get to this point! You may feel like you want to take a break or that you have done enough and will no longer have any difficulties related to ADHD. The most important message to remember is *practice, practice, practice!* This will ensure that your newly learned skills become permanent. Your effort will continue to pay off.

Homework

For this week:

✎ Congratulate yourself for completing the core treatment elements.

✎ Continue practicing skills you have learned in previous sections.

✎ Continue to use your notebook and cognitive techniques for situations involving stress.

Remember to consider any anticipated problems completing the homework.

Additional Skills

Chapter 13 | *Application to Procrastination*

This session will be helpful if you have been having significant difficulties with procrastination. For adults with ADHD, procrastination can be a result of what we call *cognitive avoidance*—deliberately postponing tasks because you can focus more easily when you are closer to the deadline. Procrastinating may also result from perfectionistic expectations for the final product.

The section on procrastination consists of a single session because it utilizes several of the skills you learned in previous parts of the treatment, including cognitive restructuring of perfectionistic expectations, breaking down tasks into manageable steps, and learning to set realistic goals for completing individual steps rather than the entire task.

Learning skills for managing procrastination will enable you to:

- Understand the attractive aspects of procrastination

- Anticipate the negative consequences of procrastination

- Utilize techniques for problem-solving around procrastination

- Use adaptive thinking skills for managing procrastination

Goals

- To continue to monitor your progress

- To review home practice of previously learned skills

- To learn about the attractive and the negative consequences of procrastination

- To adapt the analysis of pros and cons (motivational exercise) to procrastination

- To adapt problem-solving to the issue of procrastination

- To learn to use adaptive thinking for managing procrastination
- To identify areas for home practice

Review of Symptom Severity Scale

As you have been doing each week, you should complete the ADHD self-report symptom checklist. Be sure to review your score and take note of symptoms that have improved and those that are still problematic.

Score:_____

Date:_____

Review of Medication Adherence

As you have been doing each week, you should record your prescribed dosage of medication and indicate the number of doses you missed. List triggers for missed doses.

Prescribed doses per week: _____

Doses missed this week: _____

Triggers for missed doses: _____

_____

_____

Review of Previous Modules

Each week you should review your progress implementing skills from each of the previous modules. It is important to acknowledge the successes you have achieved and to problem-solve around any difficulties.

Review: Tools for Organization and Planning

- Calendar for managing appointments
- Notebook for recording a to-do list
- Notebook for breaking tasks down into subtasks
- Notebook for managing and prioritizing multiple tasks
- Strategies for problem-solving and developing an action plan
- Triage and filing systems

Review: Strategies for Managing Distractibility

- Breaking tasks down to match duration of attention span and taking breaks between tasks
- Utilizing distractibility delay
- Using stimulus control for environment (removing distractions)
- Using stimulus control for important objects (identifying specific place for each)
- Distractibility reminders (dots and alarm): "Am I doing what I am supposed to be doing?"

Review: Adaptive Thinking

- Using Thought Records to identify negative thoughts
- Review list of thinking errors
- Using Thought Records to create balanced, helpful thoughts

Many individuals with ADHD have struggled with procrastination for quite some time. In this chapter, you will review your history with procrastination and try to identify the areas in which it has been most problematic. In addition, you will learn to think about the reasons behind procrastination. Once you discover the reasons, you will be able to utilize more effective problem-solving strategies that will decrease the interference of procrastination.

The Attractiveness of Procrastination

While procrastination can cause anxiety and anguish, there are also reasons why it seems desirable or easier to postpone tasks. Some reasons include:

- Perfectionism or fear of negative evaluation for a less-than-perfect product

- The difficulty of getting started started unless the time pressure is there

- The overwhelming nature of the issue

- The difficulty of finding a starting point

- The unattractive nature of tasks that require sustained effort

- The thought that it makes sense to wait for a period when there is enough time (this usually never comes)

Do any of these reasons sound familiar to you? Think about the reasons that seem to underlie procrastination for you. Are there any other reasons that are not listed here?

As discussed, procrastination can appear to be a good option if it helps you avoid a negative feeling or if you think that the time or the environment must be just right before you can begin a task. Unfortunately, these potential benefits are often outweighed by far more negative consequences, including

- The stress of waiting until the last minute

- The fact that the task, which is unattractive in the first place, seems even worse when it is all-encompassing (waiting until the last minute means that one has to sacrifice other activities near the deadline)

- The risk of missing a deadline

- The tendency to feel worse about oneself afterward

- The fact that the final product is often not as good as it could have been

- The fact that ignoring the problem usually makes it even worse, and even harder to solve later

Do you recognize any of these consequences? Have you experienced them? Think about how procrastination has had negative consequences for you. There may be other negative outcomes that are not listed above but have been significant for you.

Skill: Evaluating the Pros and Cons of Procrastination

At the beginning of this treatment, you used a pros/cons worksheet to evaluate the merits and disadvantages to making changes in managing ADHD symptoms. This same technique is useful in understanding the overall outcome of procrastination.

Unfortunately, it is sometimes difficult to remember the pros and cons in the moment when you are facing an overwhelming task. Taking a time-out and reviewing the pros and the cons can be a useful motivational exercise to get you going. Remember that sometimes the short-term pros and cons differ from the long-term consequences, so be sure to evaluate both.

You can use this worksheet to rate the pros and cons of procrastination objectively.

Form: Evaluating the Pros and Cons of Procrastination

	Short-Term	Long-Term
Pros		
Cons		

Skill: Adapting Problem-Solving to the Issue of Procrastination

Earlier in treatment you also learned skills for problem-solving. When a task feels overwhelming or you are uncertain about where to begin, you are more likely to procrastinate. Breaking the task down into manageable steps will help you avoid this. Remember that each step should feel completely doable. If it doesn't, break the step down further. Alternatively, rather than attempting to work on the whole problem, you may want to target only one or two goals.

Another trap is to set unreasonable goals. Recall that each step should be realistic. The skills you learned for managing distractibility will also be useful here. If you know that your attention span for working on unpleasant tasks is 15 minutes, then break down each step into goals that can be completed in that time frame.

Refer back to problem-solving worksheets completed in previous modules. These exercises can be done in your notebook.

Skill: Using Adaptive Thinking to Help with Procrastination

As you have learned, your thoughts can play a powerful role in how you feel about a situation, and they can influence your actions in a situation. Negative automatic thoughts can also greatly contribute to procrastination. Using Thought Records will help you create balanced, helpful thoughts that will decrease procrastination.

Remember, there are five steps to completing the Thought Record:

1. List the situation that is contributing to procrastination.

2. List your automatic thoughts regarding the task or goal.

3. Identify your feelings connected to the thoughts.

4. Refer to your list of thinking errors to evaluate your thoughts.

5. Formulate rational response to these thoughts.

Form: Thought Record

Time and Situation	Automatic Thoughts (what was going through your head?)	Mood and Intensity of Mood	Thinking Errors (match thoughts from list)	Rational Response

Example

As you know, practicing new skills is essential if you are to be able to use them easily in a given situation. Think about a specific task or issue about which you have been procrastinating. Specifically use each of the skills we have described to help you with this task or issue. Use problem-solving to help break the task into manageable steps. Then, write down the steps in your notebook. Next, list the automatic thoughts you are having about getting started. Finally, identify the appropriate thinking errors and try to come up with helpful, rational responses.

Potential Pitfalls

Although you may struggle with procrastination for many years, it is important to remember that you can use the strategies you have learned to decrease the interference of procrastination. Even if you are unsure about whether they will help, do an experiment! For one month, commit to using these skills each day, and see how well you do. Chances are, you are going to see the results quickly, and it will then be easier to practice your newly learned techniques.

Homework

For home practice, plan a reasonable goal or two to initiate from the list of steps.

Determine a way that you can reward yourself upon completion of the goals. Then review your use of skills from the previous sections of treatment. Be sure to note any questions or difficulties you may be having.

Chapter 14   *Relapse Prevention*

Thinking About the End of Treatment

Congratulations! You are now at the end of more than a dozen chapters worth of information and skills designed to help you treat the distress and impairment of your ADHD. However . . .

The completion of this workbook, and, indeed, the end of your sessions with your therapist, does not equal the end of your program of treatment.

The strategies and skills that you rehearsed as part of this program now need to be practiced regularly so that they become automatic. In other words, the end of regular sessions of treatment signifies the starting point of your own program of treatment, in which you work to lock in and extend the skills and strategies that you have learned.

If you make practice of these skills part of your daily or weekly lifestyle, you will help ensure that you continue to maintain or extend the benefits you have achieved.

To begin your transition to this next phase of treatment—where you take over the role as the therapist, directing your own treatment—it is important for you to recognize the nature of any benefits you have achieved.

Please take several moments to review the symptom scores you wrote in at the beginning of each chapter. You may want to recopy the scores here so that you can see when and where during the course of treatment you made particular gains. Remember, the benefits from any particular treatment strategy may not appear until it is practiced for several weeks.

Form: Charting Progress

Chapter	Score
1	
2	
3	
4	
5	
6	
7	
8	
9	
10	
11	
12	
Other	

Examining What Was Valuable for You

Consider also what strategies have been most useful for you during the program. The list that follows summarizes many of the strategies you have tried.

Please rate the usefulness of each strategy to you ("0" = Didn't help at all; "100" = Was extremely important for me). Also, take some time to provide notes to yourself about why you think each strategy worked or didn't work to help you, and figure out which strategies might be most helpful for you to practice over the next month.

Form: Examining the Value of Treatment Strategies

Treatment Strategies	Usefulness Ratings	Notes About Your Application/Usefulness of the Strategy
Review: Tools For Organization and Planning		
▦ Calendar for managing appointments		
▦ Notebook for recording a to-do list		
▦ Notebook for breaking tasks down into subtasks		
▦ Notebook for managing and prioritizing multiple tasks		
▦ Strategies for problem-solving and developing an action plan		
▦ Triage and filing systems		
Review: Strategies for Managing Distractibility		
▦ Breaking tasks down to match duration of attention span and taking breaks between tasks		
▦ Utilizing distractibility delay		
▦ Using stimulus control for environment (removing distractions)		
▦ Using stimulus control for important objects (identifying specific place for each)		
▦ Distractibility reminders (dots and alarm): "Am I doing what I am supposed to be doing?"		
Review: Adaptive Thinking		
▦ Using Thought Records to identify negative thoughts		
▦ Reviewing list of thinking errors		
▦ Using Thought Records to create balanced, helpful thoughts		

Successful treatment does not mean that you will not have future difficulties with symptoms. For most conditions, symptoms can wax and wane over time.

■ *The key to maintaining treatment gains over the long run*
is to be ready for periods of increased difficulties. ■

These periods are not signs that the treatment failed you. Instead, these periods are signals that you need to apply your treatment skills. To help you refresh your skills, please use the worksheet listed on the next page. The purpose of the worksheet is to remind you of the importance of practicing skills and to help you think through which strategies might be important for you to practice in a month.

The first step in being prepared for this review is to schedule it. If you followed aspects of this program, you now know exactly where your core calendar is—it is in your picked location (and if it isn't there, this might be a first reminder to work harder to always return your important tools to your selected spot). Please schedule in a review session with yourself one month from the current date.

1.   What skills have you been practicing well?

2.   Where do you still have troubles?

3.   Can you place the troubles in one of the specific domains used in this treatment?

4.   Have you reviewed the chapters most relevant to your difficulties? (Which chapters are these?)

5.   Have you reviewed the table in which you recorded which skills were most helpful to you in the first phase of this treatment? Do you need to reapply these skills or strategies?

It may also be helpful to match some of the symptoms you may be experiencing with some of the specific strategies used in treatment. Examine the table that follows, and see if it helps you identify some of the strategies that may be helpful to practice.

Form: Troubleshooting Your Difficulties

Symptoms	Skills to Consider
Failure to give adequate attention to details; making careless mistakes in work or other activities	Recheck your attention span and your ability to break activities into units where you can sustain attention. Use your cues (beeper, dots) to remind you of core responsibilities at hand.
Difficulty sustaining attention in tasks	Check your management of your space (are your environments too distracting?).
Failure to listen when spoken to directly	Talk to others about finding optimal times for conversations, or use shorter units of talk.
Difficulty organizing tasks in terms of importance	Use your notebook and rating system. Use your triage and filing systems.
Procrastination	Use problem-solving and adaptive thinking.
Losing things necessary for tasks or activities	Use a single work area. Use your triage and filing systems. Work with another person to reduce clutter.
Becoming easily distracted by extraneous stimuli	Manage your environment, and use your distractibility delay.
Being forgetful in daily activities	Use your beeper system and your to-do list, along with your calendar.

Finally, you may want to use the problem-solving worksheets in Chapter 6 to more carefully consider any difficulties with symptoms you are currently having. If these strategies do not help, consider getting additional input from family or friends or a booster session from your therapist.

We wish you the best in applying your program of treatment.

References

American Psychiatric Association (1994). *Diagnostic and statistical manual of mental disorders* (4th ed.). Washington, DC: Author.

Barkley, R. A. (1998). *Attention-deficit hyperactivity disorder: A handbook for diagnosis and treatment* (2nd ed.). New York: Guilford Press.

Barkley, R. A., & Murphy, K. R. (1998). *Attention-deficit hyperactivity disorder: A clinical workbook* (2nd ed.). New York: Guilford Press.

Craske, M., Barlow, D. H., & O'Leary, T. A. (1992). *Mastery of your anxiety and worry: Client workbook.* San Antonio, TX: Psychological Corporation.

D'Zurilla, T. J. (1986). *Problem solving therapy: A social competence approach to clinical interventions.* New York: Springer.

Hallowell, E. M. (1995). Psychotherapy of adult attention deficit disorder. In K. G. Nadeau (Ed.), *A comprehensive guide to attention deficit disorder in adults: Research, diagnosis, and treatment* (pp. 146–167). New York: Brunner/Mazel.

Hope, D. A., Heimberg, R. H., Juster, H. R., & Turk, C. L. (2000). *Managing social anxiety: A cognitive-behavioral therapy approach.* Boulder, CO: Graywind.

Heimberg, R. H. (1991). *Cognitive-behavioral treatment of social phobia in a group: A treatment manual.* Unpublished manuscript available from author, Temple University, Philadelphia, PA.

Kelly, K., & Ramundo, P. (1993). *You mean I'm not lazy, stupid, or crazy?: A self-help book for adults with attention deficit disorder.* New York: Fireside.

Linehan, M. M. (1993a). *Cognitive-behavioral treatment of borderline personality disorder.* New York: Guilford Press.

Linehan, M. M. (1993b). *Skills training manual for treating borderline personality disorder.* New York: Guilford Press.

Mayes, V. (1998). A clinician's handbook for attention-deficit hyperactivity disorder in adults. Unpublished Ph.D.dissertation, Colorado State University.

McCullough, J. P. (2000) *Treatment of chronic depression: Cognitive-behavioral analysis system of psychotherapy.* New York: Guilford Press.

McDermott, S. P. (2000). Cognitive therapy of adults with Attention-Deficit/Hyperactivity Disorder. In T. Brown (Ed.), *Attention deficit disorders and comorbidity in children, adolescents, and adults*. Washington, DC: American Psychiatric Press.

Nadeau, K.G. (1995). Life management skills for the adult with ADD. In K. G. Nadeau (Ed.), *A comprehensive guide to attention deficit disorder in adults: Research, diagnosis, and treatment* (pp. 191–217). New York: Brunner/Mazel.

Nezu, A. M., Nezu, C. M., Friedman, S. H., Faddis, S., & Houts, P. S. (1998). *Helping cancer patients cope: A problem-solving approach*. Washington, DC: American Psychological Association.

Novaco, R. (1994). Clinical problems of anger and its assessment and regulation through a stress coping skills approach. In W. O'Donohue & L. Krasner (Eds.), *Handbook of psychological skills training: Clinical techniques and applications* (pp. 320–338). Boston: Allyn & Bacon.

Novaco, R. (1976). *Anger and coping with provocation: An instructional manual*. Unpublished manuscript, University of California at Irvine.

Otto, M. (2000). Stories and metaphors in cognitive-behavior therapy. *Cognitive-Behavioral Practice, 69,* 166–172.

Otto, M.W., Jones, J. C., Craske, M. G., & Barlow, D. H. (1996). *Stopping anxiety medication: Panic control therapy for benzodiazepine discontinuation (therapist guide)*. San Antonio, TX: Psychological Corporation.

Persons, J. B. (1989). *Cognitive therapy in practice: A case formulation approach*. New York: Norton.

Safren, S. A., Otto, M. W., Sprich, S., Perlman, C., Wilens, T. E., & Biederman, J. (in press). Cognitive-behavioral therapy for ADHD in medication-treated adults with continued symptoms. *Behavior Research and Therapy.*

Safren, S. A., Sprich, S., Chulvick, S., & Otto, M. W. (2004). Psychosocial treatments for adults with ADHD. *Psychiatric Clinics of North America, 27,* 349–360.

Van-Brunt, D. (2000). Modular cognitive-behavioral therapy: Dismantling validated treatment programs into self-standing treatment plan objectives. *Cognitive-behavioral practice, 7,* 156–165.

Wilens, T. E., McDermott, S. P., Biederman, J., Abrantes, A., Hahesy, A., & Spencer, T. J. (1998). Cognitive therapy in the treatment of adults with ADHD: A systematic chart review of 26 cases. *Journal of Cognitive Psychotherapy, 13,* 215–227.

About the Authors

Steven A. Safren, Ph.D., is the Associate Director of the Cognitive-Behavioral Therapy Program and the Director of the Behavioral Medicine Service at Massachusetts General Hospital, as well as an Assistant Professor of Psychology at Harvard Medical School. Dr. Safren maintains a clinical practice treating clients with cognitive-behavioral therapy in addition to his involvement with training and research. Dr. Safren was the principal investigator of a two-year initial study of CBT for adult ADHD funded by the National Institute of Mental Health (NIMH) and is the principal investigator of a five-year NIMH study to evaluate its efficacy. He has authored more than 40 publications in the areas of cognitive-behavioral therapy, psychopathology, and their application to a variety of clinical problems in adults. In addition to his focus on adult ADHD, Dr. Safren works on the development and testing of interventions related to medical problems such as HIV. This work is also funded by the National Institutes of Health.

Susan Sprich, Ph.D., received her doctorate in clinical psychology from the State University of New York at Albany. She is a Clinical Assistant in Psychology at Massachusetts General Hospital (MGH) and an Instructor in Psychology at Harvard Medical School. She is the Project Director for a five-year study of CBT for adult ADHD funded by NIMH. She is also involved in clinical research in the treatment of PTSD, trichotillomania, and other anxiety and mood disorders. She has authored more than 15 publications in the areas of ADHD and anxiety disorders in children and adults. Dr. Sprich conducts cognitive-behavioral therapy with clients with mood disorders, anxiety disorders, and ADHD through the Cognitive-Behavioral Therapy Program at MGH and in private practice.

Carol A. Perlman, Ph.D., received her doctorate in clinical psychology from the University of Miami in Coral Gables, Florida, and is a Clinical Assistant in Psychology at Massachusetts General Hospital (MGH), an Instructor in Psychology at Harvard Medical School, and Project Director at the Harvard University Department of Psychology. She is a cognitive-behavioral therapist who specializes in the treatment of mood disorders, anxiety disorders, and adult ADHD. Dr. Perlman served as a therapist for the initial study of CBT for adult ADHD and is a co-investigator and therapist for the efficacy study. Dr. Perlman is also involved in clinical research examining the efficacy of cognitive-behavioral therapy for post-traumatic stress disorder and bipolar disorder. She is also the project director for a study of memory of childhood sexual abuse and treats clients in the MGH outpatient clinic.

Michael W. Otto, Ph.D., helped develop the Cognitive-Behavior Therapy Program at Massachusetts General Hospital (MGH), serving as director of the program and Associate Professor of Psychology at Harvard Medical School until leaving MGH in 2004 to become Professor of Psychology at Boston University. Clinically, Dr. Otto has specialized in the treatment of anxiety and mood disorders and has developed clinical research programs for the treatment of panic disorder, posttraumatic stress disorder, social phobia, bipolar disorder, psychotic disorders, substance dependence, and medication discontinuation in clients with panic disorder. Dr. Otto's research activities are closely tied to his clinical interests and target investigations of the etiology and treatment of anxiety, mood, and substance-use disorders. Of particular interest to him is the development and testing of new treatments, including the modification of treatment packages for novel populations (e.g., Cambodian refugees). He is a federally funded investigator and has published more than 170 articles, chapters, and books spanning these research interests.